Christian Family Living

Christian Family Living

Christian
Family Living

HAZEN G WERNER

ABINGDON PRESS

NEW YORK   NASHVILLE

CHRISTIAN FAMILY LIVING

Copyright, 1958 by The Graded Press

c

To Catherine

A Troubadour of the Spirit

CONTENTS

CONTENTS

Christian Family Living

Christian Family Living

The Importance of the Family

FASHIONS may come and go. Cultures and civilizations may change. The dwelling of man may alter from a sod shack on the prairie to a ranch house in suburbia, but the family remains. Parents and children together form a corporate life of their own, unique and abiding.

THE FAMILY SURVIVES CHANGE

The family is important because it survives all change and decay. Margaret Mead, noted anthropologist, has pointed out the fact that in every known society we find everywhere some form of the family. W. E. Hocking goes so far as to say, "Where there are no families, there can be no state." [1] History reveals some deviations from the family pattern, but we find in history's length and breadth a constant reversion to the family structure. Evidently this structure has met the need for survival.

Modern Israel has established an interesting type of community known as the Kibbutz. In this community married couples live together but the children are cared for collectively. However, if accounts are true, persons living under this scheme are growing restive. For every three persons

---

[1] William Ernest Hocking, *The Coming World Civilization* (New York, Harper and Brothers, 1956), p. 11.

who join a Kibbutz, two persons leave the movement.
Usually it is the woman who instigates the withdrawal. Far
more satisfaction has been achieved by Israel in settling
refugees in villages of individual homes where normal family
life can be carried on.

Life begins in the home and for most of us it ends there.
Not many of us get very far from home, either in memory
or in the personalities we develop and take around with us
for a lifetime. So much of the home gets into the very fiber
of one's being as a child. It enters through discipline, sugges-
tion, and learning. Our memories reveal these early experiences in our development. Memories of Sunday afternoons
around the piano, the growing dusk, and the Sunday evening supper bring back a happy cluster of associations. More
important than the silver and china passed on from mother
to daughter are the memories behind them—the conditioning
that matured us. Here in this corporate home living is the
validity for much that we believe and are. "The child is father
of the man," as Wordsworth put it.

There are those who take the family for granted. A family
is a family—why write a book about it? A footnote would
do, some may say. And yet—do you remember that unforgettable moment in your life back there when you were a
little child? You went out into the darkness of the night with
your father. Together you looked by lantern light at the
fuchsia growing beside the house. Or perhaps you recall
the times when during a thunderstorm your mother would
come in and lie beside you until the thunder and lightning
had passed. These unforgettable memories alone merit more
than a word spoken edgewise in behalf of the family. Your
folks—the kind of folks they are and the life you lived together as a family—gave you your faith in God, your hold on
honesty, your ideas of loyalty.

The family has a meaning that has to do with the Eternal; a meaning that is more than sentiment about a New England door rock or a familiar curving stairway back in that old house of years ago. The family is no committee convened for a transient reason. Something of that family is in your soul. You can neither deny nor forget it. No wonder politicians try to conjure up a fireside mood that will aid them to trade on family feeling and thus induce confidence in their promises. Politicians know that the family is important. The Madison Avenue boys know it, too. They spend millions of dollars in advertising to exploit this same family feeling.

THE FAMILY IS BASIC TO SOCIETY

The family may be as simple and as commonplace as the living room, but it is cosmic in its effects. Like Greenwich time, the family is the deciding unit of existence. Why is the family so basic to society and human destiny? To begin with, in the early years of a child's life he is most suggestible. These are the years when the growing life is exposed most continuously to the influences of father, mother, and other members of the family. Parents have the first opportunity of affecting the feeling, thinking, and believing of their children.

The basic emotions—the hunger to belong, to be needed, to be secure, to be loved—are nurtured mainly in the relationships of the family. Again the family is best suited to transmit from one generation to another, ideas of behaviour and ways of living together. Here in the matrix of the family a child will learn the principles of community and the skills with which to meet life. Here a child acquires early some ideas of self-worth, knowledge that gives meaning to existence, and a faith in what abides. All of this goes on in the family.

RESPONSIBILITIES IN THE HOME

The importance of the family emerges in the responsibilities of the home. One thing is sure: Parents cannot abdicate their job. We have been farming out our children to the public schools during the weekdays, the church schools on Sundays, the guidance center for correction, and the playground for recreation. But let us know this now: The adequate, wholesome ordering of young life must come about through the home. Education for marriage and parenthood, yes! Institutional helps and psychological skills concerning child care, of course! These are aids to right understanding and practice. There is, however, no substitute for the inner spiritual forces of family life. These are evident in the example of parents as they go about the everyday affairs of living and as they purposely teach a way of life to their children. There is no way in which you can equate the glory expressed in the mathematics of the little six-year-old boy who said with all his soul, "Mummy, I love you as many times as God can count."

Modern research and social agencies will never take the place of the Christian family. When husband and wife genuinely love each another, when they truly want and love their children, when each member of the family respects and trusts the other, when together they habitually worship God at home and at church, the growing mind comes to count upon the reality of that faith for all future experiences. Modern aids to family life are needed, but they cannot be substituted for the real presence of love, faith, and respect in the home.

THE FAMILY MAKES LIFE WHOLE

The family is important because it releases forces that can make life whole. The family is a creator of those strengths that can bind societies and peoples together. Here within the orb of its intimacy you can find something that keeps the world from falling apart. It is a spirituality born out of a love that unifies all within its relationship. It is a sharing of life that reassures. It is a discipline rising out of the daily necessity of getting on together. All these make a concern for others inevitable.

In a more close-up sense, a family is that structure of living together within which the soul of a man carries on his most important earthly experiences. Here is where one's mind sets up living attitudes. Here is where decisions in reference to one another who are members of the same family, are made for lasting effects. A father may decline a better job because it would mean long absences from the children. When Christian parents accept belief in immortality because of the feeling about the imperishable meaning of loved ones, their children sense the vitality of their faith.

Here in the family the deepest experiences take place. Home is where things happen that matter most, where life hides its real crises. Here familiarity breeds contempt or contentment. Here, too, you bring your wounds from out of a world of competitive living for healing. Here is where you lay bare your depletions of body and soul. Young and old come home like clocks run down to be wound up again. Here you expose your emotional weaknesses, that through understanding you are led to find reason and courage to change. Here, too, is expressed the impassioned hunger to belong. Here character and inner depths of being are nourished

by spiritual renewal. All this goes on by divine help. It
cannot be otherwise.

ROOTS OF THE FAMILY

Certainly one can conclude that the roots of the family
run deep down in the emotions of all of us. There is a vivid
battle scene of the Civil War described by Burke Davis, in
which Georgians and Texans were rushing up to the fight-
ing line in support of their gray-clad comrades. Interest-
ingly enough, a curious diversion took place. Standing
just aside from the stream of men, a soldier waved a bundle
of mail, letters from home. For a moment men forgot the
battle and rushed over toward the soldier and crowded
around him.[2] There is a strange, magnetic power in these
family relationships of ours. No matter where we go or
what we do, there is a tie to the family life of which we are
undeniably a part.

Henry Guntrip, British psychologist, tells us, "Deep down
we never desert entirely those who gave us birth and brought
us up." Speaking of this significant emotional attachment,
he adds, "The better they are as parents, the more stable is
his personality. But however unsatisfactory they may be,
the child seems to be incapable of giving them up in his
inner mental life." [3]

In a very socially progressive state school for the correction of children, I learned that most of the children came
from homes not worthy of the name. Many of the fathers
were drunkards, many of the mothers were prostitutes.

[2] Burke Davis, *They Called Him Stonewall* (New York, Rinehart and Company, 1954), p. 225.
[3] Henry Guntrip, *Psychotherapy and Religion* (New York, Harper and
Brothers, 1957), pp. 82-83.

These were homes of poverty and filth, homes that lacked every semblance of decency. Yet the children who came from such homes would plead with the guidance officer to be allowed to return home, if only for a brief visit. Their bodies had barely healed from bruises received at the hands of a parent. Some of them were literally kicked out into the street. Still the image of home was ineradicably there.

Strangely enough, clean beds, good food, kind treatment, never eclipsed that image. The fact that the child is psychically bound to the home seems to say something quite final about the family as such. When you look at the family through the ages and in our age, you conclude that a family image inlays the life of all of us. This image of the family is psychically a part of our being.

At first glance, the life of the family seems so commonplace. After all, what is so homely as the home? Or what is more familiar than the family? But make no mistake about it, the family is the very core of existence.

Religion and the Family Belong Together

THE most important announcement of all history had to do with the family, "unto us a child is born." With this announcement, there began life's greatest family and thus, too, began the Christian faith. The two belong together— the family and Christian faith. They are two halves of the same whole. "Home and religion are kindred words," said Horace Bushnell, "home, because it is the seat of religion; religion, because it is the sacred element of home. . . . A house without a roof would scarcely be a more indifferent home than a family without religion." [1]

THE FAMILY ROOTS IN THE ETERNAL

There is a natural affinity here. Observe that the concepts of family life are rooted in the Eternal. When we speak of father and son, we know we are speaking in terms of the highest in relationships. Note the similarity to the Trinity in the concept, father, mother, and child. Paul evidently had in mind this affinity when he wrote to the Ephesians: "I kneel before the Father from whom every family

[1] Quoted by Andrew W. Blackwood in *Pastoral Work* (Philadelphia, Westminster Press, 1945), p. 84, from Horace Bushnell in *Christian Nurture* (New Haven, Yale University Press, 1916).

18

in heaven and on earth derives its name and nature, praying Him out of the wealth of his glory to grant you a mighty increase of strength by his Spirit in the inner man." (Ephesians 3:14-16, *The Holy Bible, A New Translation* by James Moffatt.)

In one of his letters to a friend, W. Forbes Robertson spoke of family life as the highest life we know. He suggests that the father, son, and family life on earth is a faint picture of something better in heaven. Someday he thinks we shall be surprised to find that the noble and divine for which we have been searching has been with us all the while in homes that are Christian.

Religion and the family belong together. Here is history's greatest identification. They complement each other, as the two blades of a pair of scissors. Religion and the family are as indispensable to the work God is doing in our midst as the sun and the rain are necessary to growth, beauty, and the harvest. We know that awful desolation, scarred earth, and starved lives result from years without rain. We know, too, the certainty of decay, disease, and death when there is no sunshine. Religion and the family work together, thus making possible the moral and spiritual growth of persons and society.

The family, by reason of its very structure, makes inevitably for an alliance with religion. The intimate quality of family life, the profound interdependence of its members, the nourishing sense of its oneness, the nature of its responsibilities—all these reveal something of the family's need for religion.

Religion is a redemptive force which is to create sound character. It seeks to establish the relation of sonship with God as the Father. It maintains the Ecclesia—the fellowship of believers. If we are willing to grant that these are purposes of religion, then surely we must grant that these purposes can best be accomplished in partnership with the family.

RELIGION NEEDS THE FAMILY

We have been talking about the natural identity of religion and the family in the growing of Christian persons. Note the place of the family in this partnership. Religion is native to the family. Religion is familial. The family is the incarnation of the Divine. We believe that God took upon himself the limitations of human existence, and came among us so that we might know him. That incarnation was an event within a family. How amazingly we come to know him in the heightened experiences of family life.

To begin with, we see this fact of the incarnation in the sacredness of marriage. At its highest, marriage is a rarefying, spiritual experience. Again, we sense the presence of the Eternal in the mystic and divine act of human birth. God is strangely near and real to parents when a child comes into their home. God is present in the eternal nature of the love that persons within the family feel for one another, as they grow up together and venture out into life. There is no other love like it. "For the family," said W. E. Hocking, "is the most direct embodiment of human love; and human love is, in its own complete self-consciousness, inseparable from the love of God. It is the natural context for a sacrament, inasmuch as it is by way of human love that the divine is most frequently and concretely discovered." [2] These heightened experiences that move so deeply within us are inseparably a part of the experiences of God as Father. The family is the incarnation of the divine.

[2] William Ernest Hocking, *The Coming World Civilization* (New York, Harper and Brothers, 1956), p. 130.

The family is important for religion. It serves an important function as it engenders religion in the growing culture. The spiritual truths that children experience so naturally in the home become just as naturally an abiding reality for them in the ongoing years. Boys and girls have learned many of the great verities of our faith in their homes. Theologians may write, exhort, and explain the doctrines of our religion. But it is the children who grow up in homes where the highest we can know takes place that will continue to say, "This I know because I have experienced it as a member of a Christian family."

This great power in the family which presses upon us the nature of great spiritual truths can work also in the opposite direction. Leslie Weatherhead tells about an interesting letter he received. A woman wrote to him saying that she always "feared God because she was told as a child that when there was a thunderstorm, it meant that God was angry with her." [3] Thus a little child developed a needless fear that warped her relation to God even as an adult.

A positive understanding of the Christian faith at this point of belief begins in the home. We feel something of the immanence of God when we are in the presence of a father and mother and their newborn child. We learn about immortality in the experiences of the family. Immortality lives in the very nature of the family. Mrs. Clarence Hamilton speaks of her husband's reaction to the tragic death of their daughter. She adds, "But to Don came also some new ideas, from his pondering on life and death and time. 'Nothing,' said he, 'can take my wife or children from me—neither life, nor death, nor things present nor things to come, nor height nor depth nor any created thing. This I know, if I

[3] Leslie D. Weatherhead, *Prescription for Anxiety* (New York & Nashville, Abingdon Press, 1956), p. 44.

know anything. There's something everlasting and eternal about a family like ours, and I guess right now I've thought for the first time about eternal life.' " [4]

We learn something of the self-giving of Jesus when we watch a mother exhausted and weary, staying on at the bedside of a sick child. In such an emergency she refuses to be concerned about her own need for rest. We learn something of the compassionate forgiveness of the heavenly Father by experiencing the care of an earthly father.

A small boy had been consistently late in coming home from school. His parents warned him to be home on time on a particular day. Nevertheless he arrived at his home later than ever. His mother met him at the door but said nothing. His father met him in the living room but said nothing. The family went in to dinner. The boy sat between his father and mother. He looked over at his mother's plate and saw meat, vegetables, potato, and a cup of coffee. He looked up at his mother but she said nothing. He looked at his father's plate and there again he saw meat, vegetables, potato, and a cup of coffee. He looked at his father but his father said nothing. The boy looked down at his own plate and there was a slice of bread and a glass of water. The boy was crushed. There was a moment of silence which seemed endless. Suddenly the father took the boy's plate and placed it in front of himself. Then he took his own plate and put it in front of the boy as he smiled at his son. When that boy grew to be a man, he said, "All my life I've known what God is like by what my father did that night." Experiences like these bring us early the realization of great spiritual truths.

[4] From *Our Children and God* by Mrs. Clarence Hamilton, copyright 1952, p. 60, used by special permission of the publishers, The Bobbs-Merrill Company, Inc.

In the family we find the best possible occasions for guiding the growing religious experience of children through prayer. We talk about the need for prayer groups. We go about organizing such groups. All the while the family is a made-to-order prayer group. The symmetry, the coherence, the close-up life of the family makes for an astounding spiritual facility in nourishing and cultivating experiences of prayer. If there is any doubt about this assertion, just imagine for a moment that our nation has been conquered and is under the control of a godless regime. Imagine our Christian faith in the desperation of such a time being driven underground. If ever our Christian faith is driven underground, it will survive in the family—not in individuals as such, but in members of families. The family has perpetuated itself for centuries and has gone on maturing the forces of its own survival. If our Christian faith is ever forced to nourish its life in secret, it will live on because the family will not be able to live on without it.

The family is important for religion in the implementation of its character ideals. There is a certain finality about the family. If what we need is a better public morality, a reconstructed humanity, a universal peace, a revival of evangelical religion, then we had better turn to the home. Where else but in the family is there such help? There we find the strongest reason to live right, not to let one another down, and to be what we should be. When you get down to it, what the gospel of Jesus demands morally and ethically of individuals, every father and mother actually want for their growing children.

The need of religion for the family is not difficult to establish.

THE FAMILY NEEDS RELIGION

The modern American family needs to deepen its life in the will of God. Within the family the members—their hopes for one another, their ideas of behavior, their sense of to-getherness—need to deepen their relationships in the eternal. James Mutchmor describes the grounding of the Delphine Dodge, a million-dollar yacht, in a fog off Manitoulin Island. Despite her large crew, her radar equipment, her gyro-compass, she went on the rocks. That same night in the same fog, a man who was Mutchmor's friend brought his little fishing tug safely to the harbor. All this friend possessed was a compass, an old alarm clock, and a stub of a pencil with which to keep his reckonings. Someone asked, "How did you do that?"

He said in substance, "That was easy. What was hard was getting out from behind some dangerous rocks the preceding February in a howling gale and snowstorm."

Again the question, "How did you do that?"

He replied, "Well, I know the floor of this lake better than the contours of this land. Give me five or six sound-ings and I can reset my course and make the harbor." Mr. Mutchmor continues his account, "Out of the depths Captain Ed Purvis got his directions." [5]

The modern family may have all the equipment that modern mechanization can make possible, but it needs to get its guidance from out of the depths of the abiding and ultimate truth of God. Ideals of sound Christian character, the prac-tice of genuine respect one for the other, the satisfactions of the desire to belong—all these call for the light that God can give. Here is a mother who never ceases to hold her boy up to God in faith that he will speak, live, and act

[5] James Mutchmor, *The Christian Gospel and Its Witness* (Nashville, Tid-ings, 1955), pp. 38-39.

according to the highest. The same boy, now a young man away from home, continues to live under the influence of that early conditioning. Faith in God, so much a part of his childhood, provides him with abundant reason not to let his family down.

There is no disputing the fact that as an entity, the family needs its own spiritual renewals. There is a family consciousness of such—a corporate life that needs inner restoration—if its purposes are to be fulfilled. "Whom God hath joined together"—not only man and wife, but through them all who are within the home—God can keep together. He alone can preserve the spiritual wholeness of the family. When a family is at one with God, it comes about that God's love is at one with the love of each member of the family for the other. Thus their relation to God makes their common security more real and meaningful. Religion is important to the home. The family cannot go it alone. Differences of mind, misunderstandings that crop up, continued illness, or even boredom, can cause a family to let go at the seams. You need something you can believe in and live by as you live together in a family. Those virtues of generosity, mercy, and patience, so necessary for the healing and help that must come to the family, will need to be of a spiritual size great enough to accomplish these ends.

The Christian faith is important to the family in trouble. Fearful and frightening things can happen to the family and to the members of it. Terrible cruelties occur at times in the home. Oddly enough, there are those individuals who often give the worst to those they love the best. How can you resolve these hostilities, impositions, and torments? What about the tragedies that visit the family? In the vigil of bleak nights at the bedside of a loved one there comes an awful

sense of loneliness when that loved one dies. For that loneliness the only healing comes from God.

A family needs direction. A family needs the direction of
a God whose presence they can feel in the home. John
Charles Wynn says, "Those parents whose Christian maturity
has enabled them to find their way to God-in-Christ can
possess a self-acceptance and a depth of understanding that
are valued above mere techniques of child management, or
even those newly popular skills of group relations." [6] The
modern family is growing weary of a way of life whose only
answer to family needs is a scuff-proof floor wax, or the
promise of more leisure, or a development housing with no
payment down. Members of the modern family want to
know how they can keep together, how they can give security
to all within its bounds, and how they can preserve this
wonderful family love. The modern family is beginning to see
that these values are based upon eternal truth and power.

It happened at church that a family was transformed, made
able, victorious. This particular family faced the obstacle of
more than one hostile circumstance. They had to cope with
a background of ignorance, wrong living, ill health, and un-
employment. It was a large family with many mouths to
feed. Before this vital religious experience members of this
family drank, cheated, and swore. Then came the awaken-
ing, and their acceptance of Christ. I carry in my memory
a picture of that baby carriage in the hall of the church.
It is a sign of the loyalty of these folks who were always
there at worship. With this new life many new problems—
economic distress, illness, and trouble on every hand. I saw
that family come through victoriously, and it was their Christian faith that did it.

[6] 11 Questions for Key Parents (Published by the Board of Christian Education of the Presbyterian Church in the U.S.A., Philadelphia, Pa., 1957), p. 8.

On Being Christian
in the Family

CHRISTIAN growth rests unmistakably upon the Christian family. You can worship in church, you can be an accountable Christian in business and society, but nowhere is the living of our religion so under the white light of reality as in the family. Is there any other kind of religion than the one that is lived? Is there any place where the living of one's religion is so put to the test as in the home? Here all that one means by being a Christian can be woven into every moment of life. If you are really a Christian, where will it be so unalterably plain as in the way you meet the unpleasant incident within the home? It is also quite apparent in the attitude that you display before your children when you face a neighbor's unwarranted hostility. In your feeling about your daughter's friend who does not measure up to your standards, you reveal the quality of your Christian living. It shows too in your reaction to your boy's repeated lying.

WHAT IS A CHRISTIAN HOME?

To come to the point, what is a Christian home? Does it mean that every member of the family professes the Christian way of life? Is it that the family prays together at a definite time each day? Does it mean that all members of the family

27

subscribe to the same Christian beliefs? Or that every member of the family is a member of the church? Perhaps! At least these are some of the norms by which people judge whether or not a family is Christian.

Consider this definition. A Christian family is one in which the presence of Christ is known and acknowledged by each one in the home. Trust in God is a daily experience on the part of all. An attempt is made to bring each member of the family into the Christian way of living. The Christian family gives thanks at meals and engages daily in prayer. Parents accept responsibility for the instruction of the young in the fundamentals of Christian living and character. The family develops in each member a Christian outlook in respect to the people of the neighborhood, the nation, and the world. And again, a Christian family provides abundant desirable activities and many wholesome books and stories that are suitable for growing boys and girls.

Add to the above conception these characteristics of a Christian family:

(1) Parents are conscious of a divine vocation in the rearing of their children.

(2) Older members of the family by example make valid a trust in God and the practice of the way of Jesus.

(3) Conversation in the home is in keeping with God's spirit and is a part of the total Christian stewardship of the life of the home.

(4) Life in the home makes room for and gives encouragement to individual meditation.

(5) Membership in a family that believes in and recognizes the divine worth and dignity of persons becomes the natural inheritance of every growing mind.

All that has been said above may be condensed into this one sentence from the booklet of the First National Methodist

Family Life Conference: "The Christian family recognizes its relationship to God and its obligations to serve him."

The Christian family as described here may seem too difficult, too formidable, to attain. Nevertheless let it be said that a family purposing to live the Christian way can attempt no less. If a family does not accept the way of Jesus, translated in the terms of family living, wherein does that family differ from secular families? There are many people all about us who really want to know. What difference does it make in the experiences of marriage? How does it affect a parent's discipline of his child? When a family is Christian, what difference does it make in their understanding of sex? How does Christianity influence family goals?

John Charles Wynn quotes Paul Calvin Payne as saying, "Having a Christian home means far more than a houseful of nice people who treat each other fairly kindly and who go to church fairly regularly. It means a home where Christ is known and loved and served; where children come to know him through their parents; where Christian training of the children is placed ahead of the social ambition of the mother and the business ambition of the father; where the father is determined to carry on his business in conformity with the mind of Christ; where both Father and Mother are determined to make their social life conform to high Christian ideals; and where eyes see far horizons of a world to be won for Christ." [1]

A CHRISTIAN FAMILY DESIGN

But how is the family to go about living the Christian way? A Christian family is a family that lives in accordance with

[1] From *How Christian Parents Face Family Problems* by John C. Wynn. Copyright, 1955, by W. L. Jenkins, The Westminster Press, p. 15. Used by permission.

a Christian design. The Christian family does not just happen. It grows out of a reasoned and accepted way of life—Christ's way of life. There is an architecture of living about the Christian family that is distinctly different. The Christian family lives in such a way that it expresses Christian hope, guidance, and love. It places all of its life in harmony with the purpose and will of God. The Christian family lives by an intelligent and dedicated plan. That plan is reasonable and joy-giving, because it holds to Christian values and Christian assurances through God's love and care. The family lives by and for this Christian design.

The really significant feature of this design is that God is supremely important in the life of every member of the family and in the life of the family as a whole. In many families the importance of God is a matter of something we say in church. How important is God to the life of your home? How much does he have to do with what is important to you as parents? You undoubtedly are responsible parents and you love your family and home. How significant is your relation to God? Are your minds and lives filled with little things like the slope of the driveway that makes it almost impossible to get in and out of your garage in the wintertime? Are you thinking most about the stock at the supermarket, or the meeting of the P.T.A. nominating committee? Perhaps you have questions about Jimmy going to the party or you wonder if Harvey's watch is worth repairing. Even in the midst of all these details you need not lose sight of God.

CONVERSATION IN THE FAMILY

If God is important to the home, isn't it altogether likely that what he means to each member of the family will find its way into the conversations of the home? At any rate, conversation on the part of the family ought to be consonant with God's love and law. What we talk about at the table or in the living room has meaning for all of us as a family. Unless religion is just a Sunday morning habit, certainly faith, love, fair play, truth, the essentials we live by, will come into conversation naturally. If they are really religious, as families discuss what they see on television, what happens on the highway, the discoveries of medical science, the present communist threat, they will realize that these are matters of concern to God. Their faith in God and their personal consecration can help them discover relationships.

In the Christian home, conversation will naturally be geared with the spiritual. Dr. W. T. Thompson tells us that "a number of graduate students at the University of Chicago, when asked where they got their major ideas in morals and religion, replied, 'Through the conversation in our family at mealtime.' " [2] What a different picture is presented by Anna Laura and Edward W. Gebhard, who quote a college student as saying, "All Dad cares about is making money, and he doesn't care too much how he does it, either. Oh, I know Dad would be shocked to hear me say that. He'd probably like to have me think that what he cares most about is being chairman of the church board of trustees. But you should hear him talk when he sees a chance to make an extra dollar—even at the expense of someone else!" [3]

When the family lives by a Christian design, all that goes on in the lives of the family—their distresses, expectancies, unfoldings, disciplines—all are experienced with God. The family that lives this way has strength. Such a family meets every situation, the rebelliousness of a child or the unforeseen

[2] W. Taliaferro Thompson, *An Adventure in Love* (Richmond, Virginia, John Knox Press, 1956), p. 136.

[3] Anna Laura and Edward W. Gebhard, *Guideposts to Creative Family Worship* (Nashville, Abingdon Press, 1953), pp. 43-44. Used by permission.

shock of a serious accident, with a grace and firmness that come from God.

A Christian design means the adoption of Christian aims. Christian parents hold the highest in character and behavior before their children. One young man wrote home from college to his father. He said that having come of age, he thought he would take up some of the things that other men around him were doing. He specified what these things were. He ended his letter by asking his father's advice. That minister father wrote thus to his son: "You are of age, and you have the right to do as you think of doing. It's up to you. But the one thing that I want to say to you is this: 'Not any of these things is in the picture of the highest life that you can know.'"

A CHRISTIAN IDEA OF SUCCESS

A Christian design also yields a Christian concept of success. Christian youth growing into adulthood learns that in economics, the major question for him is not "How much?" but "What?" and "How?" The Christian design calls for faith, good sense, and a Christian ethic. The Christian concept of success sees achievement in terms of usefulness and resulting character. For Christians satisfaction and fullness of life come not primarily from financial gain, but from holding to honesty and truthfulness, and being loyal to Christian ideals. A Christian design commands individuals to regard other persons not for what they have, but for what they are. In the secular world how you get what you want is not so important as how much you can gain. For a Christian how you get it is the important thing. A Christian family therefore needs to keep constantly before growing children the meaning of spiritual and ethical values. The great bequest of the Christian home to its children is living according to the highest they know—the life and teachings of Jesus Christ.

God has his way in a Christian home. The total life of such a home from the beginning, at the time of the marriage, is founded upon God's will. Too many people get married, start a home, buy a house, set up a way of life, fashion their goals —taking for granted that God wants what they want. Instead families need to be sure that life in that home is what God wants it to be. How do you know what God wants for your home? Did you ever ask him?

CHILDREN IN CHRISTIAN HOMES
GROW SPIRITUALLY

The great business of the home is to develop sound persons for a useful and happy life. In the Christian home children are to grow spiritually while they are growing physically and mentally. As a child grows in successive adaptations to his surroundings, in knowledge and in the handling of all relationships, he should be growing also in an understanding of God, and in right and useful living. No matter what else parents may do they should provide homes in which they consciously make opportunities for the spiritual growth of their children. Otherwise their children will remain underdeveloped spiritually.

As parents you make sure of physical development through obedience to the rules of health and participation in athletic activities. You see to it that social development comes through lessons of politeness and good taste. You encourage activity at gatherings for children and young people. You make sure of intellectual development through vigilance about homework and grades. You plan a college education for them, but what are you doing about the spiritual growth of your

child? Are you helping him to discover within that feeling of
"ought," that sense of moral obligation? Do you help him
learn a regard for the rights of others?

What are you doing about his prayer life? Is the prayer
experience of your boy at night just routine and occasionally
amusing? Or have you through daily comradeship helped him
to enter into an experience of spiritual growing in that sacred
moment before he goes to sleep? How wonderful it is when
your boy learns to bring before God in prayer all the hap-
penings of the day that are important to him and to his life.

The end of the day is your opportunity to orient your children to the spiritual world! For a little while you can talk over
all that took place—the mishaps, the funny things, the proud
successes, the little failures. Let the children bring all these
into prayer as you explain that God will understand and help
us to make a better start tomorrow. Perhaps your boy pushed
the flower pot off the window ledge. Someone threw a stick
at his dog and injured him. Your little girl was tempted to
cheat in the classroom. Perhaps the misfortune came about
through a broken doll. How wonderful when all of this is
lifted up for cleansing and renewal, for understanding and
encouragement, and for the healing of the hurts. As you help
your child to bring all the events of the day together with the
feelings of defeat, of culpability, of wonder, of questioning,
openly before God, you are helping him find the way into
ever enlarging life. When this happens your child is growing
spiritually.

And then, there are the other children in far places of the
world; many of them are without food while we waste it; they
may lack adequate clothing or shelter. Let us bring all these
needs before God while a small child asks him to bless the
children in other lands. There is no better beginning of a
conviction concerning world missions. A child grows spiritual-

ly in an astonishing measure when the spiritual life, vital and vivid, pervades the mood and culture of the home.

The Family Can Achieve a Happy Life

The Christian family is one that achieves a happy life. It is important to experience the fact that the Christian family is a happy family. If there were more happy Christian parents, there would be more Christian growth in our homes. W. E. Hocking once said that children are inclined to adopt the beliefs of people who are happy.

Of course every family has its moments of elation. It isn't difficult to sail with the breeze. These climactic experiences are good for a family. Promotion, a salary increase, first prize in the exhibit of canned fruit at the fair, a daughter or a son cast for the chief part in the school play—these are some of the things that bring gladness to the family. But what about the experience of the family between times, in all of the commonplace days of living together? Is it a mood of ennui that settles down on the home? Is the family enveloped in a bleak mist most of the time?

There is a spiritual indwelling, a vast reserve of well-being, in the Christian home that ill-fortune cannot repress, nor tragedy extinguish. That's the difference in a Christian family. There is always that restoration of courage and hope in the presence of God.

True happiness on the part of a Christian home is not banished by adversity. We are not speaking here of joking and laughter. We are referring to the kind of happiness that comes into the life that confesses God's love and rests upon his illimitable care. Happiness for the Christian is based on that which will never pass, on that which will go on and on because nothing can ever defeat it. There is no extinction of it. It's the happiness that exists when two people love each other with the kind of love that lights up all that is ordinary or routine. It's the happiness that comes about when the family knows itself eternal through the grace of God by the gift of his Son.

This happiness of the Christian family is like the happiness of St. Francis of Assisi. He laid down everything—clothing, possessions and wealth—in his father's shop. He wrapped about him a piece of burlap sacking, tied it about his waist with a piece of discarded rope, and went out into the night under the frosty sky to sing his song of trust in God.

There are families that must keep up a wild tempo in order to induce gaiety and a pleasurable feeling. There are families who rely on drink to lift up their spirits. One couple said, "It worries us that on almost every social occasion, people serve liquor as though it were necessary to lose some of your senses in order to have a good time." "We don't need liquor," they said, "to be gay. Life is always a matter of gaiety in our home."

A Christian family is one that achieves an abiding, lasting happiness.

4

What Parents Should Know

THE taproot of reality in the Christian family is the recognition of the sacred meaning of each person in that intimate relationship. Out of this realization comes the flowering of respect for one another that makes familial love so fragrant. Without respect, love itself becomes a pitifully feeble thing. It is hard for us to realize how fundamental this principle is.

BEING AN EFFECTIVE PARENT

A small boy stood in front of the lost-and-found desk. The eyes that peered over the top of the desk gave unmistakable signs of tears as he made his inquiry: "Has any mother been turned in yet this morning?" Evidently a mother was desperately needed. They always are. So are fathers. The search is on for good parents—understanding parents—parents who know how to help their children become mature Christian persons. And apparently parents do want to know, judging by the hundreds of questions parents across the country are asking as they participate in discussion groups on parent-child relations.

How is a parent really to know? Does a certificate of fitness as a parent come with the birth of a child? No! In this greatest

37

of all vocations, many parents go about their task in a hit-and-miss fashion. Parental fitness is the result of genuine concern, seeking, and application. Many articles in magazines written by people proficient in the field will offer considerable wisdom in child care. Innumerable books have been written for parental guidance. An encyclopedia of child care, when published, was described as containing "everything a parent needs to know before birth to adolescence." Anyone would be quite credulous to believe that claim. Data and light gathered out of investigation, studies made by experts, and the actual experiences of families will prove useful.

Perhaps there is virtue in some very simple rules. Here are a few of them: (1) Be consistent. When discipline is inconsistent, a child is never sure of the kind of behavior that his parents expect. Gushes of affection interspersed with unreasonable reprimands or frequent neglect will produce a "jerky," unstable, and uncertain adolescent. (2) Refrain from, "When I was a boy. . . ." After the first hundred times, these words have about as much influence as a worn-out record. (3) Avoid nagging. It does not help. It's a sign of weakness. It is better to discipline the child for wrongdoing at the very time it is done, and then drop the matter. Don't nag at him. (4) Deal sincerely with your child's questions. When Georgianna comes asking a question or help, avoid waving her aside with "some other time." If the present is not suitable, set a definite time for a talk.

Much that parents need to know is not found in books, magazines, or courses of study. Parents do need to know something of the functioning of personality, the processes of emotional and social growth, the influences of our secular culture upon the growing life. However, in spite of the importance of knowledge in the more scientific or exact sense, we need to recognize that there is no substitute for the ability and willingness of parents to share in the everyday life of their children. Nothing is more important than the attempt of fathers and mothers to be mature persons and the integrity that results from living what they believe and teach.

Someone will say, "What is the difference between Christian parents and parents who do not practice this way of life?" Whether or not parents claim to be Christian, there still remains the necessity for them to acquire some knowledge of child growth and care. There is no magic whereby a Christian parent comes to understand all about personality development and the emotional needs of children. They must work to discover the kind of parental reactions that make for normality and fullness of life. The Christian parent, however, uses his knowledge within the framework of God's purposes for each person within the home. He acts with a conscious concern for the sacred meaning of each person within that intimate relationship. The Christian parent experiences reinforcement that comes with the knowledge of being a part of God's creative work in the family.

A Christian parent who is consciously practicing the Christian way, may by that fact have the grace to be patient a little longer. Such a parent tends to be somewhat more sensitive to spiritual as well as to emotional needs of growing children. They are better able to administer discipline out of the conviction of the inescapability of God-given moral laws. The Christian parent conscientiously tries to be an example of honest and truthful living. The best description of the maturity we strive for in a modern Christian home is found in these New Testament words, "And Jesus increased in wisdom and stature, and in favor with God and man."

PARENTS BEING WHAT THEY ARE

The greatest influence for the good life of your child is you. Fritz Kunkel used to say that education is not so much a matter of the education of the educatee, as it is a matter of the education of the educator. The personality of your child is to an astonishing degree a question of you. The maturity of your child is mostly a question of your maturity. The freedom from anxiety on the part of your child is largely a matter of freedom from anxiety on your part.

For example, the genuine love of parents for each other as husband and wife has much to do with the confidence and security which their children feel. More than one study has revealed that parents, unhappily married, are prone to be hard on their children. Where there is no love lost between husband and wife, it is not unusual for the wife as mother to deluge her child with affection. The father may withdraw into himself and have little part in the life of his wife or child. When this occurs, it has a traumatic effect upon the emotional life of the child and the parents. The absence of happy unity on the part of the parents causes children to feel unsure. Such a situation threatens the security and confidence that children need in their growing years. Children who grow up in an atmosphere of quarreling, jealousy, hostility, and bickering often find it difficult to form mature relationships when they become adults. The unsureness that comes with the years takes its toll as long as they live.

Yes, what you are determines what your children will be. This happens because emotional learning on the part of children comes through absorption—a kind of pedagogy by contagion. What you are makes its impress upon the unconscious life. It isn't just what you say that registers with your child, but more importantly, what you feel as you say it, how you really feel toward him. How else account for the fact that a child knows when he is not wanted? In spite of the outward affection lavished upon a child by a parent who is inwardly frustrated and burdened with a sense of guilt, his child knows things are not right.

The child feels, more than consciously knows, the indifference that is all too poorly disguised by a show of kindness. The discrepancies in adult behavior, the rationalizations of his parents, the untruth ever so plausible, the jealousy badly veiled do not escape him. When parents are concerned over the conduct of their son only because of what the neighbors will think, he senses that after all he is not very important to his father and mother. In the emotional learning of the child's growing life, what is real makes its impress.

Whether you know it or not, as a parent you are being put to a stiff test. You have to be a real Christian; no ersatz kind of religious life and practice will do. John Charles Wynn asks, "What difference does it make which Bible stories we tell them at bedtime if they see us living daily as if we had never opened the dust-covered Book?" [1] This author refers to an incident in George Bernard Shaw's *Misalliance*. A demanding and domineering mother compelled her child to learn the Sermon on the Mount. Actually she was teaching quite another lesson, namely, that the mother herself was not Christian.

Much that a child becomes is due to unconscious imitation. Oddly enough, many of the mannerisms of a father are passed on to the boy through unconscious imitation. He becomes in some respects the echo of his father's personality. He walks with the same kind of peculiar swing, he clips his words in the same fashion, he inclines his head slightly to

[1] John Charles Wynn, *How Christian Parents Face Family Problems* (Philadelphia, Westminster Press, 1955), p. 16.

one side, even as his father does. So great is the power of a parent that the admonition to be honest, given ever so emphatically by the father, gains scant attention. Why? Because the memory of an incident in which a traffic ticket was torn up and discarded refutes what is being said.

Benjamin Fine, who made a study of 2,500 students, found that three fourths of them did not consider lying or cheating wrong. They gave as the basis for their feeling, things that their parents had done, such as smuggling in perfume and doctoring up income tax reports. There were other students, however, who said, "Thank God, my father and mother brought me up to know what is right and what is wrong."

Jesus indicated what he thought ought to obtain in all human relationships when he said, "Love thy neighbor as thyself." He had in mind that both persons in any given relationship are sacred.

CHRISTIANS IN THE FAMILY
RESPECT ONE ANOTHER

A respect for one's self, as well as a respect for others, is all-important in successful and responsible mutual living. Indeed one must love himself aright to know how to love his neighbor aright.

With some reluctance, a woman in the interview room who had come for help unfolded the disturbing story of her husband's gradually increasing abuse. He was a good man in many ways. Why did this happen? It began with slighting remarks made about his wife in the presence of others. He seemed to be obsessed with the idea of finding fault. A constantly growing disdain fed the fires of his hostility. Finally physical abuse followed this deterioration of the love they once knew for each other. The marriage tie eventually became unbearable. The wife was more to blame than would appear on the surface. If you permit another to degrade you, you are contributing to the degradation of yourself and the other person. Any wife or husband has a right to insist on respect for personality. Personality is as sacred for one as for the other.

Husband and wife, mother and father, need to bear this principle in mind. If they discipline themselves in the early stages of compulsive hostility and stop short of ridicule and nagging, they can save their marriage. The constant realization of the sacred worth of the other person and the continuous practice of respect are the only vital deterrents to wrong attitudes and practices.

In the Christian home, the practice of respect rests upon reverence for persons. All of this adds up to the spiritual reasonability of the shared life in the home. Let there be no superior person or persons. Family living is like a bridge in the eastern part of our country, where five roads converge. There traffic must merge into a single lane to move across the stream. Courtesy and the recognition of each person's right to his turn facilitate the matter of travel at this difficult point. In the same way, a family council can be the means of facilitating a consideration of everyone's opinion within the family circle. Together the family can arrive at a common mind and decision. Someone asked a thirteen-year-old boy, "What do you think makes a happy family?" He summed up his answer to this question in these words: "A happy family reminds me of a baseball team with Mom pitching, Dad catching, and the kids fielding, and with everyone taking a turn at bat."

A Christian home is a home where persons live a shared life; where decisions are made by concensus of the minds of the whole family. Every member has something of worth to contribute.

Dr. W. T. Thompson records an interesting conversation with the president of a college. The president was recalling "an experience he had with his father the day before he left for college. His father invited him to take a walk with him. 'Well,' he thought, 'Dad will now lecture me on the temptations I shall face at college, drinking and gambling and sex. He will talk to me about studying hard, living up to the opportunities for self-improvement and being helpful. He will urge me to be honest and faithful to every duty.' He rather dreaded the experience. But to his surprise the walk was a pleasant one. . . . His father was a wise man. Looking him straight in the eye, his father said, 'Son, I just want you to know that whatever happens your mother and I trust you.' That was all. It was enough! That boy determined then and there, with steel wrought into his will, that no matter what the cost he would never violate such trust. He never did!" [2]

Part of our trouble lies in the fact that dominance is not always evident outwardly. Tyranny in the family can be a very subtle thing. Some years ago, a boy of fifteen disappeared from home. He was not found for months. When all the facts were known and the case history established, one could not discover a flaw. The home was regular and normal. The father had given attention and time to be with his boy. The boy had worked on Saturday, earned a bit of money, shared it with his sister. He was not an introvert. He had been identified with all the boys in the games of the neighborhood. These were the facts, and yet the boy had fled from his home. Why?

Lurking beneath it all, he felt that he was in a straight-

[2] W. Taliaferro Thompson, *An Adventure in Love* (Richmond, Virginia, John Knox Press, 1956), p. 129. Used by permission.

jacket. He wanted to escape it. Without fully realizing what was motivating him, he wanted desperately to be himself.

When we respect the personality of a child, we see him as an individual. Grant those rights and privileges that belong to him. Never belittle what a child says; never ridicule his idea or expressed desire. Feelings are the same size for every person at every age level. A child is not a being who will become a person some day when he grows up to be like you. A child is a person now.

A CHRISTIAN FAMILY PRAYS

The family at prayer is a family with power. Where is prayer more potent than when the family lifts its united heart to God? There is something of spirituality unalloyed when the "two or three gathered together in my name" are a family united for the purpose of finding God's guidance into a larger life.

Think of all that can and does happen as the family prays. There is a deepening sense of solidarity. There is confirmation of the home as having its own God-directed vocation. There are impressions of the family relations as lifelong and eternal in nature. Deposits of ill-will that have gathered during the day vanish and in their place is a satisfying sense of affection for those near and dear.

In all of this experience of prayer, the child in the home has the refreshing feeling of security. He develops a feeling and purpose that makes him determine never to let God down and never to let his family down.

The members of the family come before the throne of grace daily empowered to forgive one another.

Through prayer the family grows in religious living. Each person grows spiritually in integrity, in insight, and in grace.

Children Are Persons

THE attitudes of parents and other adults determine to a great degree the concepts a child forms of himself, of life and of God. A recent study of twelve-year-old boys in Ohio was made in the area which had the highest delinquency rate. It was found that 101 of these boys were considered potentially delinquent. In this same high delinquency area were twenty-five boys who had not come into contact with the police and the court.

The interesting fact was this: (1) The potentially good boys had "socially acceptable or appropriate concepts of self and others," and their mothers and teachers concurred in these judgments. (2) The potentially delinquent boys had adverse concepts of themselves and others. The mothers and teachers of the delinquent boys concurred in the adverse opinion these boys had of themselves. A child in whom there is maturing an adequate self-concept and the resulting strongly structured life can resist the deteriorating influences within a community.

Evidently what you feel or think about your child has much to do with what he feels or thinks about himself. What you do to your child in the way of frustrating him evidently results in his own self-frustration. If, for example, you treat him as inconsequential, tell him over and over that he'll never amount to much, you are helping him to build that kind of self-concept. Eventually he will live up to it.

Observe what this means in religion. A child who has never known the full and real love of parents will find it hard to trust completely in the love of God. Leslie Weatherhead says, "Children have so often been made to feel that their parents will not love them unless they are good that they inevitably project on to their heavenly Father the feelings they have developed about an earthly father and mother. . . . They cannot believe in UNCONDITIONAL LOVE, but only in a love which depends on the attainment of moral standards. . . . The glorious truth is that God loves us whatever we do and our 'rights' are the rights of a love-relationship, that of sons and heirs, not the right born of achievement in the moral realm." [1]

LOVE YOUR CHILDREN

The simple, homely virtue fundamental to the happy maturing of the life of your child is love. Someone asked a mother, "Do you think all children deserve the full and impartial attention of the love of a mother?"

"Of course," she said.

"Well, which of your children do you love the most?" the inquirer asked, hoping to catch her in a contradiction.

"The one who is sick until he gets well," she answered, "and the one who is away until he gets home." The love felt for one another in the family—this is the fulfillment of God's plan. "Every one that loveth is born of God."

At a Family Life Conference, something emphatic was said concerning the need of full and free parental love. One woman who was in attendance said to the person sitting next

[1] Leslie D. Weatherhead, *Prescription for Anxiety* (New York and Nashville, Abingdon Press, 1956), pp. 45-46. Used by permission.

to her, "This may sound strange, but the first thing I am going to do when I get home is to call my little girl into the living room and tell her that I love her. I've never done that. I've been a pretty frigid and cold mother. I was brought up that way. There wasn't any love in the home that I grew up in, and I guess it just became a part of me."

Genuine parental love, naturally demonstrated, comes nearer to being the cure-all for all the problems of child care than anything else that one could possess. Your love as a parent is most important to your child at the very moment when he is least lovable. This parental love is as needful to the spiritual and emotional growth of the child as food is to the body.

Ardis Whitman in her recent book refers to the work of Dr. René Spitz, a New York psychoanalyst. He spent three months observing the reaction of babies in a foundling home where "the nursing staff was so busy that each child, as he put it, 'had only one-tenth of a mother.' " Dr. Spitz estimates that "30 per cent of the babies actually died before they were a year old. 'Without emotional satisfaction, children die,' says Dr. Spitz. 'Emotional starvation is as dangerous as physical starvation. It's slower, but just as effective.' " [2] "There can be no question of the fact," says Dr. John G. McKenzie, "that to be loved and to love does give that sense of belonging to someone, that sense of security which is necessary to the possession of confidence. Without confidence we cannot face life." [3]

Parental love must be a love for the child's sake. When parental love is real, it is a love that wants happiness and fullness of life for the one loved. "Infantile love," says Erich

[2] Ardis Whitman, *A New Image of Man* (New York, Appleton-Century-Crofts, Inc., 1955), pp. 115-16.

[3] John G. McKenzie, *Nervous Disorders and Character* (New York, Harper and Brothers, 1947), p. 102.

Fromm, "follows the principle: 'I love because I am loved.' Mature love follows the principle: 'I am loved because I love.' " [4] Mature love means that a mother or a father is ready to share in the life and growth of the child, and to release the growing person into the ever-enlarging orb of existence.

Unless the child is loved for himself, he withdraws into himself. His need of love unmet causes him to try to live as though he had no emotional needs. His emotional life is thus repressed. Two hundred British girls, aged fourteen and fifteen, were asked to tell why they thought a hypothetical "Mary" loved her parents. They replied as follows: 66 per cent said that the parents cared for her; 40 per cent said the parents helped and guided her; only 8 per cent replied that it was her duty to love her parents. [5]

Subtract parental love from the parent-child relationship, and the child lacks the feeling of acceptance. Here is the great danger. For this lack, the home today must bear its share of blame for delinquency in this country. Without parental love and the approval and acceptance which it implies, a youngster lacks a sense of self-worth. He feels frustrated in his desire to belong. For him it is as though he had been shut out and not wanted by those who should have stood by him.

A study was made of the twenty-one G.I.'s who went over to communism after the Korean War. An analysis of that study revealed some plain reasons for this defection. Nineteen of these twenty-one felt unloved or unwanted by fathers or stepfathers. Sixteen had withdrawn within themselves. Eighteen took no part in school activities or sports. Only one was

[4] Erich Fromm, *The Art of Loving* (New York, Harper and Brothers, 1956), pp. 40-41.
[5] From "Family Life," February, 1956, a monthly service bulletin of The American Institute of Family Relations, edited by Paul Popenoe.

ever chosen by his classmates for anything. It is quite obvious that we have here more than a lack of patriotism. The roots of the weakness of these boys run deeply into early life. Home and society must accept its share of the blame.

LOVE THAT IS NOT LOVE

There are parents who condition their love upon a child's good behavior: "Mother won't love you if you aren't good"— "If you aren't a good little boy, I'll just give you away." According to Dr. Henry Guntrip, "When the child comes to feel that he is only loved for conforming, obeying, being polite and good and 'nice,' that he is only loved so long as he is suppressing his own vital challenging individuality and letting himself be stamped with the pattern of other people's demands, he loses hold on himself as a real person." [6]

There are parents who condition their love on a child's willingness to please. Children grow up trained to the one chief aim of pleasing their parents. The mother lavishes affection on her children when they do what pleases her. She is aloof or angry when she is displeased with what they have done. When she withdraws her love on such occasions, she lets her child down in such a depressed state of feelings he may respond in very undesirable ways.

Parents sometimes exploit their children as a means of nourishing their pride. The precocious child is often the victim. In one instance, a father and mother fussed and fawned over their child, prompting him to make smart remarks. They looked about to make sure that everyone was noting the clever things he said. "He is so far ahead of every other child we can't leave him in school," the mother boasted.

[6] Henry Guntrip, *Psychotherapy and Religion* (New York, Harper and Brothers, 1957), p. 114.

"He doesn't play with other children," she went on, "they bore him to death." This child was a curiosity, an exhibition, a child without a chance. His parents were betraying him, as unfit parents often betray a tiny, helpless life.

Any child is defenseless against his parents. Take a television quiz program. We catch a glimpse of the parents of the phenomenal child sitting in the front row, looking on triumphantly. However, we are disturbed by the tense, strained look on the face of the child. Any child is defenseless against this inordinate pride of parents. The need for importance on the part of the parents may be satisfied, but the child will bear emotional scars for the rest of his life.

There are parents who are perfectionists. Children are pushed by parents to excel in athletics, to keep ahead in school grades. It is unwise to force your child to strain after the stars. Children lose confidence in themselves and in life when they consistently fail to meet their parents' expectation. They end up with deep-rooted inferiority feelings. This kind of perfectionism can only result in devastating frustration.

There are parents who continuously compare a younger child with an older sister or brother. A younger child who grows up under the shadow of a brilliant brother or sister has a hard time of it. It is unfair and injurious to hold up the superior abilities of these older members of the family in order to coerce a child to perform as parents want him to perform.

The important thing is to love this child of yours because he is yours. You love Johnny not because he knows all the answers, not because he plays the clarinet well, not because he is getting good marks, or has an unusual vocabulary. You love him because he is Johnny. You love him for himself and because he is yours. In all the world there is no security which can compare with that. With a love like that comes a sense of belonging, of being needed, of being sufficient. That's how a child grows up to be a sound, mature person.

PATTERNS OF PARENTAL CARE

There are unwise patterns of parental care that need to be examined from a Christian point of view. They may be accountable for the emotionally and spiritually underprivileged children of today.

OVERINDULGENCE: "I have had a hard struggle in my life. I'm going to see to it that my children have it easier." Nobody can dispute the kindness that may prompt such an assumption. However, the wisdom of it is certain to be subject to dispute. When parents overshelter or overshadow their child, the result is likely to be a partially developed personality. One finds in either instance the lack of the very security that is so much desired.

Henry C. Link quotes the confession of the young man who said: " 'I have failed in business, I can't hold a job, and now I can't hold my wife. I have lost most of my friends and I can't even hang on to my money. I have had every advantage,' he admitted, 'because my parents denied me nothing. They paid for my expensive college education, and they set me up in business. When I fell in love, they financed our marriage and our home. They did not want our marriage to suffer because of money worries. But now my marriage and everything else are ruined. I don't know where to turn. Everything has been done for me. I have about decided that there is something radically wrong with me.' " [7]

You may, say, "I don't want my child confronted with

[7] From *The Way to Security* by Henry C. Link. Copyright 1951 by The Reader's Digest Association. Copyright 1951 by Henry C. Link, reprinted by permission of Doubleday and Company, Inc., p. 23. Used by permission.

what is unpleasant, laborious, or distasteful." By shielding your child from every difficult and trying circumstance, you rob him of the natural right to face life. He needs to face life and to be confronted with the necessity of choice-making; out of the latter comes growth and maturity. You can't do your child's thinking or concluding for him, but you can help him to achieve the right and the good. And when he does, he is more certain to try to do the right and the good another time. He may find what is true by your help, but he must practice it for himself. One little girl said, "The trouble is, they expect me to do what they want their way, while I've got to do what we both want—my way."

POSSESSIVE LOVE: "That love that possesses," says Peter Bertocci, "is the love that destroys more than it creates." Isn't it strange that the mother who gives life can also take it away? We've all known mothers who are very uncertain as to whether any girl is good enough for her son. There is the widow who implores her daughter not to marry and leave her alone. The possessive mother gets along quite well while the child is small. The trouble starts when growth continues and the young person begins to reach out to life to form new relationships.

Examine the consequence of possessiveness. When a mother completely dominates her child's life and treats him as a perennial infant, he has little chance to escape the dwarfing of personality. His life is like that of a seedling that unfortunately springs up too close to a large full-grown tree. All of its life it is so overshadowed and so cramped that there is no room for the extension of its branches. Because of this constant frustration, the growing person becomes totally dependent. In all probability, a child growing into adulthood will seek a mate whose life bears this same characteristic, who gives promise of the complete care that by now has become utterly necessary. Edward A. Strecker, the psychiatrist, reports that during World War II there were 2,400,000 young men found to be psychoneurotics who were the victims of clinging and domineering mothers.

DISTRUST: The distrustful father, whose own life has been marked by rejection, is an authoritarian kind of person. "Do as I say and don't ask why." Out of his joyless, lonely, and misunderstood childhood, this parent is on the defensive and is utterly unable to chance love. He is unapproachable, and rarely if ever says anything that shows approval of his child's conduct or attitude. He will demand implicit obedience, and maintain with his child a purely conventional relationship. One boy, who became a criminal later, said, "The only time my father ever talked to me was when he was gonna whip me. I don't think he ever loved me because he's the same way I am—he's never felt love." [8] The one time this boy, who later became an outlaw, felt emotionally overcome, was when his mother approved of something he did. Dominance by distrust leads to a history of resistance on the part of the child—a growing resentment about life. Eventually you have a person hostile to the boss of the shop as well as to the laws of the land.

A Christian parent, out of divine resources and with a will to provide for a child's individual growth, will love a child for himself, as a person. As a Christian parent try to create in the home itself a proper context for the development of your child, a strong selfhood useful and free. The most rigorous job in the world is being a parent. You have a life on your hands—a growing, changing, unfolding life. The greatest challenge that life can give is yours. With God's help meet it!

---

[8] Croswell Bowen, *They Went Wrong* (New York, McGraw-Hill and Company, 1954), pp. 112-13.

6

Parents As Teachers

THE church school has been, and is, one of the greatest agencies for the education of persons in Christian living. Men and women with incredible devotion and understanding and skills have faithfully taught the children and growing youngsters through the years in classes organized by the local church. There is a desperate need for more trained teachers. There is, however, even a greater need for understanding and dedicated parents as teachers.

When one considers the new, modern perils in the social context in which youth must live, the strange and complex influences of our secular society, it simply must be said that the church school cannot win out singlehanded. No longer can any father and mother in blissful confidence delegate the Christian education of their children exclusively to the church school. We are told that the cowbird lays her eggs in the nests of other birds to be hatched; and the birdlings are reared by these foster parents. Just so, many mothers and fathers have been allocating the Christian education of their children entirely to church-school teachers. These parents think of religious instruction as being required for the development of their sons and daughters, but they don't even know the name of the teacher of their child.

Paul H. Vieth, in an article entitled "Christian Nurture—

Then and Now," says, "Parents have been allowed too easily to assume that sending a child to church school was equivalent to providing him with religious education." Dr. Vieth maintains that "The Church which will dare to assume that the family is basic in religious education and which will refuse to accept pupils in its church school unless parents agree to carry on with the home program, will find itself not only growing in effectiveness, but also in number."

The church must begin now to enlist the home in the enterprise of religious instruction. We do need trained teachers in the church school, but we just as desperately need trained and devoted parent-teachers or co-teachers. Parents must be challenged and committed to supplementary teaching. To the parent it needs to be said: you brought a child into the world, you brought a soul into the world. At baptism you promised to teach this child religion. This child was born into your home and is your trust. "Lo, children are an heritage of the Lord."

CHURCH AND HOME

The fact is that you can't grow Christian character in thirty minutes on Sunday morning—not in the face of all the deteriorating forces so alive in today's social scene. You cannot help but be disturbed about juvenile delinquency when you consider the result of recent research. A study based on a sampling representative of the entire Protestant delinquent population of a large metropolitan area reveals these important findings: 85 per cent of those who were delinquent had attended church school regularly or occasionally; 54 per cent had joined the church, and almost two thirds were from homes where one or both parents were church members.[1] Church schools can no longer succeed by themselves.

A half-hour of Sunday-morning teaching must be integrated with seven days of experiencing, learning, and practicing religion and Christian behavior under parental guidance. This is the only plan that can ensure spiritual growth as a part of the total development of the child. It is not easy for a person to achieve personality in our complex society with its modern moral and ethical hazards. The task is too colossal for any one religious educational agency to assume. The Christian education of children today becomes a more profound problem than in the days of the past. That problem is related to the emotional nature as well as to spiritual nurture of children. The garment of sound life must be virtually hand-woven. The home is being summoned to do the weaving.

There are those who openly avow that we ought to abandon the church schools as having failed, and turn to the home as our hope. They say we ought to put all of our resources and all of our genius to work in the training of parents for the total education of the child, spiritually and morally, in the home itself. It is true that the time has come when church-school teachers can justifiably declare the futility of the church-school program unless the parents of boys and girls can be enlisted to co-operate responsibly in the Christian development of their children. For us to permit parents to go on assuming that if they enroll their child in a church school, they have done their part, is simply to let them stand on false grounds.

I knew of one church-school teacher who determined to know the parents of the children he taught. He called in each

[1] Data from Guy L. Roberts, *The Religious Backgrounds and Attitudes of 150 Protestant Juvenile Delinquents*. Unpublished Ph.D. thesis, University of Pittsburgh, 1952.

home to invite all of them to be present on a given Sunday. He wanted them to see the church-school class in session, to observe what procedures were being followed, and what Christian education was attempting to do for their children. In one home he was invited in by the father who was alone in the house. During the course of the conversation, the church-school teacher asked the father to attend the class session the next Sunday.

"Oh no," said the father, "I am really too busy for that. You just go along. I know you're doing a good job of it. I am glad that George gets to Sunday school every Sunday." He dismissed the whole matter in that fashion.

This teacher then went on to do something quite daring. He said, "You know, I am in desperate need of a car just now. My car is laid up in the shop. I wonder if you would lend me your car for an evening or two so that I can finish this calling." Immediately the father bristled up. He told this teacher in no uncertain terms that he never permitted anybody to drive his car.

The teacher replied, "No, you wouldn't let me have your car, but you'll let me have your boy every Sunday morning and you are not even interested enough to find out what we are doing with him over at the church."

It was a pretty rough way to go about it, but I am sure that father thought twice about the matter of the Christian education of his child, and what he could do about it.

There are leaders who believe that the church school should require the co-operation of parents as a condition for enrolling their child in a church-school class. When parents commit themselves to co-operate with the church school, it has far-reaching effects. There are leaders who believe that the church school should exclude children unless parents commit themselves to this teaching co-operation. The spirit

of Christian education, however, ought not to be one of exclusion but of inclusion for the sake of a richer life and
stronger character of the child. One plan that has been
offered is to enroll the entire family in the church school
as a unit, recording the various ways in which each person
is to be related to the Christian education program.

THE FAMILY AS A TEACHING CENTER

Family life offers a peculiarly apt situation for teaching.
"Nearly every Protestant denomination," says John Charles
Wynn, "now relates its church-school curriculum in greater
or lesser extent to the home. Slowly they are returning to that
pattern of Reformation days when the Christian education
of children was centered by the hearthside. Martin Luther,
who constructed his catechism to be taught by parents, was
convinced that 'the home is the God-ordained place for training in Christian character....' " [2] The family is an all-around-
the-clock occasion for learning. The lessons of trusting in
God, of being honest, of loving one another, have a constant
appropriateness in family living. Crucial situations, as
well as the little troubles that arise, cannot be kept until
Sunday for interpretation and understanding.

The spirituality which is so naturally a part of Christian
family living makes a natural setting for spiritual learning.
Religion need not be an import as far as the home is concerned. God can be readily known and felt as a presence in
the Christian home. Reasons for depending upon God are so
continuous in a Christian family that children have abundant
opportunities for learning of his love and care. What a mar-
velous atmosphere for the teaching of religious and moral
truths!

[2] *11 Questions for Key Parents* (Published by the Board of Christian Education of the Presbyterian Church in the U. S. A., Philadelphia, Pa., 1957), p. 6.

Since the family is a corporate existence, there are, in all of the experiences of its closely knit life and intimacies, unusual opportunities for practicing Christian ways of getting on together.

Parents are, by the very nature of the deep and abiding love for their children, the very persons who should be identified with the processes whereby these same children grow spiritually and morally. Parents can offer definite validity for the very truths they are enlisted to teach. They have felt the pressing necessities of faith. They have needed divine assurance so often. They have found their way to the Mercy Seat daily for their loved ones. By reason of all this, they can speak convincing words concerning the spiritual verities that the church school seeks to make known to them.

The Christian family helps each child to have a knowledge of himself as a person. Through the Christian family comes the realization of the sacred meaning of birth, likewise the feeling of self-worth. Where but in the family are such forces so likely to create a mood that makes the learning of spiritual truths so natural?

In the Christian home statements about uprightness, clean living, and noble character get into the emotional bloodstream of a child. How many times someone has said in your presence: "My father always said to me . . . ."

Parents have the greatest opportunity of all in offering their lives as a daily example that confirms what they say about living together as Christians. I remember that small boy who came home from school one noon upset and fuming mad at another boy in his class. Immediately upon coming into the house, he said to his mother, "I am certainly going to give Billy what's coming to him this afternoon. I'm sure going to give it to him." His mother could see that he was unusually disturbed and angry. She tried as a Christian mother will, to explain that a fight wasn't the best way to settle disputes or trouble. She went on finally in her endeavor to say that Jesus would go about it in a better way. He wouldn't use his fists on another person just because he had felt unjustly treated. Quick as a flash, Jimmy said to his mother, "Can you think of anyone else who would do that?" The mother had no answer.

Children are helped immeasurably by example. John Redhead tells about the experience of a friend who visited an art gallery in Athens. While there he observed an interesting thing. There was in the room a marble statue of an athlete. The friend of Dr. Redhead noticed that after walking up to the statue and peering at it intently, the tourists invariably straightened up. They threw their shoulders back, and stepped more sturdily.[3] An example has a great influence.

WHAT PARENTS NEED TO KNOW

One of the essential factors in working out this plan of parents as co-teachers is the education of the parents themselves. There is a great deal of skepticism as to whether or not parents will make a better job of it than teachers. But that isn't exactly what we have had in mind. We believe that through guidance and training, these parents can supplement the work of teachers. An important step forward would be meetings of parents and teachers. This opportunity for informal discussion would make for common mutual understanding. Parents and teachers together would discover what is needed and how parents and teachers can work together.

As a minimum requirement parents need to be able to answer the simple and direct questions that children ask. There isn't anything wrong with saying to that ten-year-old

[3] John A. Redhead, *Learning to Have Faith* (New York and Nashville, Abingdon Press, 1955), p. 24.

son of yours, "I don't know, but we'll find out." Don't brush off your child, thinking that he'll forget the matter he seems to have on his mind. At least take your boy and girl seriously when they ask, "Why can't we see God?" or "What is God doing now?" Someone has said that children are growing up when they start asking questions parents can answer. But it's precisely at these earlier years that you'll need to face questions, honestly and seriously.

You will have to be equally forthright about questions regarding sex. Be grateful that your boy or girl is coming to you instead of to other persons. Outsiders sometimes give information about this area of living in physical life that does great harm. No person will do better work in sex education than parents who, free of fear or personal embarrassment, tell the truth in plain and simple language. They need to present clearly the Christian view of sex.

In a study conducted in England, based upon 6,251 answers to questionnaires sent out to English women, some interesting facts were discovered. Among women born after 1934, one half did not ask their parents about the "facts of life," and of those who did, one half felt they were told neither the truth nor all they wanted to know. Education regarding sex may be technically correct, but spiritual connotation is essential to the teaching. Only so can children develop a sense of the God-given aspects of sex that, again and again, have significance for the young person who is growing toward maturity.

It may be well to remember that you don't tell a six-year-old boy all that is to be known about sex at one time, any more than you would try to teach him geometry when he is barely ready for arithmetic. He needs to accumulate truth about sex life as he matures. The secret certainly in this realm of sex instruction is to reveal this part of our life in terms that are positive. Adult-conceived mores forced upon the emotional sensibilities of a child often mean conformity without intelligent choice. These negative pressures experienced in childhood make for character by fear, shame, and a sense of guilt. Particularly is the latter true when there have been occasions of stern reprimand, which implied that sex is something with which you do not deal in any way. The result is that in later years, the child grows up to be good because he dares not be bad. Granted that this is one reason for being good, it certainly is not the best one. In such a negative process there has been no growth in moral understanding, since there has been no intelligent approach to moral and biological law.

Look at this matter of positive teaching and guidance in points that are kindred to this question of sex. A child should learn a love for honesty that makes stealing unthinkable. Just in the same way a child should learn a love for chastity. We can achieve this end when we help children to learn that conduct which is cheap and common can ruin a happy and useful life. Sex can be understood not just as something not to do, but as a part of life that God meant to aid in the enriching and ennobling of personality.

Erich Fromm has said, "At the age of five or six the child has acquired an all-pervasive sense of guilt because the conflict between his natural impulses and their moral evaluation by his parents constitutes a constantly generating source of guilt feelings." [4]

Walter Stokes says, "The time has arrived in our social progress when parents should make a serious, active effort to prevent a wall of fear and embarrassment from growing between their children and themselves as to matters of sex." [5]

[4] Erich Fromm, *Man for Himself* (New York, Rinehart and Company, 1947), p. 156.
[5] Walter R. Stokes, *Modern Pattern for Marriage* (New York, Rinehart and Company, 1948), p. 96.

UNNOTICED EMOTIONAL LEARNING

Again, parents need to know this important, underrunning principle in the Christian education of their child. His growth in character is going on imperceptibly all the time. Learned responses that make for wholesome, Christlike life are a matter of unnoticed growing. "A good man," says Jesus, "out of the good he accumulates, brings out the things that are good; and a bad man, out of what he has accumulated, brings out the bad."

How important it is that parents understand that doing is a large part of this learning. Jack Mendelsohn reminds us of Aristotle's words: "Men come to be builders by building, harp players by playing on the harp; exactly so, by doing just actions we come to be temperate; and by doing brave actions, brave."

The supplemental work to the church's program of Christian education should begin on Sunday noon at the dinner table, while parents talk over with the child the lesson taught that morning. In fact, it would be well to have in the hands of parents a résumé of the lesson taught. As they review it, they'll be prepared to carry forward the Christian education process from that point. Many parents recognize the value in studying next Sunday's lesson with their child. Thus parents are to take up the task where teachers leave off. Also they can help their children to prepare for the next Sunday. Often parents can initiate activities that will help to accomplish the purpose of the lesson in the lives of their children.

A child grows in tolerance by actually trying what is taught about race. He grows in love by dividing the apple and giving the larger part to a sister and feeling good about it. All of which will make it more likely that he will try it again. The lessons on Sunday morning are to be recalled and then applied during the entire week. This is sound learning.

After all, you can't do a thing by just knowing it. Teaching is to expand from the function of truth explained, to truth being lived. Through explanation validated by experience, there comes about an understanding which is deeper than just intellectual knowledge. Donald Bell quotes a coed as saying, "I can't recite the Ten Commandments which I learned in my home, but somehow, I still live by them."

In the church-school class, your boy learns about the right. If he agrees with what is taught about the right, he believes this to be the way to live. But not until he has practiced the right through your guidance and in your comradeship does he really know it. When you as the parents help him to feel the pleasure in anticipation of doing the right, and when he feels this sufficiently to forego an immediate pleasure of the wrong, he is really learning and growing.

How Is This to Be Accomplished?

It would be most unrealistic for one not to recognize the problems in a program of parent co-teaching. A number of questions must be faced. Are parents ready to undertake such teaching responsibilities? What will you do about the fact that not all parents have either the same general education or the same religious backgrounds? Further, how can you help parents of children at various age levels?

No one has a right to say that a parent-teacher plan is simple to achieve. It will call for application on the part of parents, a willingness to know, a desire to give time to the necessary training, and a readiness to commit one's life to the end of Christian accountability in the work of child development in Christian living.

Growing Mature Persons in the Family

THE greatest business in the world is the growing of sound persons in the family. What we do about this may well determine the destiny of all of us.

EMOTIONAL GROWTH

The unobserved daily growing in a given direction is one of the really important facts about life. You grow to be what you are. You have to work your passage to strong character. According to Benjamin Fine, one of the editors of *The New York Times,* society has found that juvenile delinquency is not a sudden isolated incident. A child doesn't go bad suddenly and without cause. It's the daily, undeterred growing in a given direction that is important. Here is the inner technique of personality achievement. No one is born noble, any more than he is born a scholar. Richard V. McCann says, "The 'criminal in the kindergarten' can be a reality and not just a figure of speech." [1] No one built slums—they just grew into what they are. Slowly but surely, a life becomes a strong character or a person of deteriorating principles. Walter Pitkin has put it like this: "As people grow older, they grow more and more themselves." One day you are what you have

[1] Richard V. McCann, *Delinquency: Sickness or Sin?* (New York, Harper and Brothers, 1957), p. 100.

been doing and thinking a long while. Think about your own child in respect to his growth in a given direction. What is happening in his life through childhood days and adolescence? Has it been one continuous round of rationalizing, self-excusing, duty-shirking, self-seeking? If so, this is the kind of adult you can expect. The net result cannot be anything else but a self-centered, immature person.

If you could study in particularized detail the lives of boys and girls who have gone astray, it would help you to understand in some measure how character comes to be what it is. If you could see these lives in some kind of flash-back fashion you would begin to recognize how important the day-by-day choices are that a child makes. Your own choices in relation to your child would take on new significance. By an unbroken continuum of choices, your child grows a good or bad character.

David E. Roberts tells the story of a medieval blacksmith who took immense pride in his work. In fact, he put a special mark upon everything that he made. At one time a hostile army took over the town where he worked. They put the blacksmith in prison and bound him down with heavy chains. Since he was such a powerful man, he felt confident that he could break the chains that shackled him. He was sure he could find a weak link somewhere. Then he would break the chains and gain his liberty. He examined the chain, link by link, and there he found the secret mark that was the sign of his own workmanship. His heart sank in despair because he knew that there would be no weak link in that chain.[2] We grow into the kind of persons we are out of all our accumulated experiences. The choices we make throughout our lives determine the kind of persons we become.

[2] David E. Roberts, *The Grandeur and Misery of Man* (New York, Oxford University Press, 1955), p. 53.

ARRESTED EMOTIONAL GROWTH

The emotional growth of a person can be arrested. Some individuals are like apples picked green to ripen off the tree. Persons who lack emotional development suffer from personality deficiencies. "You are only young once, but you can stay immature indefinitely."

When is an adult not an adult? A person is not an adult when he compares others to himself and always to the disadvantage of the other person. An individual lacks maturity when he is unable to sustain a vital interest. When others disagree with his personal opinion an immature person takes it as a personal affront. The years have really nothing to do with being an adult. It isn't a question of the calendar. In fact, position in life has nothing to do with it. A fifty-year-old senator can have tantrums as well as a five-year-old boy. Religious profession in many instances fails to prevent this strange deficiency. A person may be an indubitable Christian in both concepts and loyalties, but a child in behavior.

Children who have been unhappy, resentful, and insecure carry their emotional poisons from these unfortunate experiences into adult life. They have on their hands a life disordered with guilt feelings. They meet each day with undue aggressions, evasions, and feelings of being inferior. They defeat God's purposes for them. Often behind the exterior of adult life are little boys and girls living in adult-sized bodies. The basic need for a successful marriage is emotional maturity, says Dr. Paul Popenoe. Divorce, chronic alcoholism, and other social failures have their origin mainly in the emotional immaturity of people.

EMOTIONAL MATURITY

In a very interesting series of articles concerning some imaginary visitors from Mars to America, a reporter in one of our great papers quotes one of these visitors as saying, "I also know how to meet disappointments with aplomb. I know how to meet injustice, how to ignore things that should be ignored, how to notice things that should be noticed. I know how to be alone, I know how to be taller than things that happen to me." That testimony may not have been intended as such, but it describes maturity quite well. According to a recent story, a teacher was depicting the hardships and sufferings of the Pilgrims. While she was telling of the starving conditions, one of the children broke in to say, "I wish my Mom had been there. She always knows just what to do."

So much has been said about emotional maturity. What is it? Here are a few of its many possible measurements. Note the implications for the growing life:

(1) Do you have the ability to stay with a job and struggle through it until it is finished?

(2) Are you willing to postpone an immediate pleasure for the sake of a future good?

(3) Do you have the kind of self-discipline that enables you to work under authority and to work co-operatively with others?

(4) Do you have a capacity for self-criticism without suffering from self-disdain and loss of dignity? A boy wrote to his dad about the football game his school had lost the week before. He said, "We lost the game. The opposing team found a hole in our line, and I was that hole." He faced his responsibility, and courageously acknowledged his own failure.

(5) Are you able to accept either blame or fame without self-injury—to learn a lesson from blame and to grow in humility when the crowd is cheering you on?

(6) Do you refuse to betray a confidence when that

betrayal would gain for you the attention that is given to one who bears important news?

If you can answer "yes" to these questions, you have a right to feel that you bear many of the marks of a mature person.

It is not difficult to see that these behavior traits that have just been mentioned form a precise picture of adequate discipleship. Jesus very ably described the mature life in these words, "Therefore whosoever heareth these sayings of mine, and doeth them, I will liken him unto a wise man, which built his house upon a rock: And the rain descended, and the floods came, and the winds blew, and beat upon that house; and it fell not: for it was founded upon a rock. And every one that heareth these sayings of mine, and doeth them not, shall be likened unto a foolish man, which built his house upon the sand: And the rain descended, and the floods came, and the winds blew, and beat upon that house; and it fell: and great was the fall of it." (Matthew 7:24-27.)

A child who grows up in a Christian home begins with great advantages that help him achieve maturity. Children in the Christian home have an opportunity to know the immeasurable love of God. They know that God forgives us, understands our limitations, and loves us in spite of sin or wrongdoing. When boys and girls experience this kind of relationship to God, they grow up with a feeling of self-worth that cannot be achieved in any other way. They do not need to feel inferior. Nor is there any necessity for such a child to build up his ego by demanding attention or by insisting upon having his way in everything. A child begins to have a sense of self-worth because of God's love for him, and furthermore he is free now to love others. There is no longer the necessity to resent or envy other persons to the point that it results in injury to his emotional life. In the Christian family the natural experiences of trust in God bring securities that are priceless.

WHAT CAN PARENTS DO?

There is no need to feel hopeless about this strange, intricate world of the emotions. There are some simple principles to observe in order to help the emotional growth of your child. Help your child to find himself, to know himself, and to know his capacities for living. You can help him to appreciate the significance of his inner life and to know that God is near. Help him to make the wonderful discovery of himself as a person. When he does this, he will discover something of his own self-worth. This child of yours has an innate desire for self-worth and approval of others. He wants to know that he means something to you, that he is important to others. He sizes up thoughts and attitudes of his parents and others toward him, and the way he feels about it has far-reaching effects on the kind of person he becomes.

He has a keen desire to be needed, a desire to belong. You undoubtedly have felt like a stranger when on various occasions you have been with groups of people. Then suddenly, out of some circumstance, unforeseen, you have the feeling of belonging, that your life has meaning to the people all around you. In some such way a child finds himself satisfied and secure within the family. Within the life and intimacy of the family he finds his selfhood. Parents can help the child to develop this sense of selfhood by letting him, under your guidance, think, plan, discover, and decide many things for himself. Insights by which he grows into this selfhood must be his own. You cannot give him all the answers. You cannot bear the bruises and the brunt of life for him. These things he must experience. They are his, indi-

vidually, even though you may share with him your love and
understanding. "One can say over and over to oneself," says
Leslie Weatherhead, "'I am loved, understood, forgiven, and
accepted.'" [3] That is the important thing in every child's
life. A mother had promised her little girl, Jane, that she
could select her own winter coat. When they got to the
store and looked over the coats, the matter resolved itself
into the necessity of a decision between a blue one and a
red one. The red coat really attracted Jane. The mother,
however, could not resist the temptation to put her judgment before the choice of the little girl. "I think I'd like
my little girl best in the blue coat."

Jane, who was still eager to have the red coat, said, "But,
mother, remember I belong to me, too."

Help your child to know himself as a person. You can
lead your boy or girl to realize that this inner self can be a
part of an indestructible order cared for by an accountable
God. With this realization comes an important self-discovery.
The growing person can then begin to realize with Herbert
Farmer this truth about God: "His is a love that goes out to
all persons, merely because they are there as persons."

Help your child to manage his disappointments and dis-
illusionments. Help him learn how to absorb the stings of
unpleasant experiences. Maturity demands a "fairly high
level of frustration tolerance."

A child must learn how to handle many kinds of things: the
unfriendly attitude of someone at school, his own feeling of
jealousy over the new baby, and the unhappiness he feels
because he was not chosen for a part in the school play.
Parents need to develop the art, the skill, and the power to
know what to do in relation to factors that are against their

[3] Leslie D. Weatherhead, *Prescription for Anxiety* (New York and Nashville, Abingdon Press, 1956), p. 30.

child. You can learn to handle situations in such a way that the experience can contribute to your child's development. This is the great essential.

Russell Davenport was in World War I. It was said of him: "His war letters began as a boy's but ended as a man's." [4]

In *The Spanglers,* a novel that concerns itself with the Civil War, you will find this statement concerning one of the characters: "As his body grew thinner, his soul seemed to lose its baby fat."

Someone has suggested that the best timber can always be found on the northern side of a mountain. Help your child to acquire some competence in overcoming hostile and hurtful situations. No life can be wholly free from them.

FOR THE COMMON GOOD

Help your child to live life for a larger significance than himself, for something beyond himself. Help him to free himself from himself through a greater devotion. When all is said and done, the substance of immaturity is nothing other than plain, common selfishness. Begin early to let go of your child. Help him to become more and more a part of life and of others. There is nothing but tragic unhappiness for the person who interprets all that happens around him in terms of how it affects him. How foolish for anyone to try to compel life and others to adjust to him and to his needs. Call this egocentricity or whatever you like, selfishness such as we have been describing is a consequence of our emotional immaturity. There is no Scripture that yields more of the light of psychological truth at this point than the words of Jesus when he said, "For

[4] Russell W. Davenport, *The Dignity of Man* (New York, Harper and Brothers, 1955), p. 4.

whosoever will save his life shall lose it: but whosoever will lose his life for my sake, the same shall save it."

Begin now to condition your child, to see all that happens in terms of how it affects others as well as himself and how it relates to the common good rather than just to himself. The time to redeem a life from self-centeredness is now, not later. When the four-year-old says, "Look at my new shoes," it is a mark of acceptable egocentricity. When the forty-year-old says, "Look at my new car," with the same infantile concern for attention, it is far from acceptable. Happiness comes to persons as a result of finding the way to a larger life—life that is lived for a reason, which in turn will bring deep and satisfying meanings. Help your child early to lose himself in absorbing interests and work that result in good to others. When he gives himself to a wholesome cause that brings benefits to more than himself, he experiences an important phase of truth.

The most glaring sign of immaturity is self-centeredness. There is not much maturity in saying, "Why did this have to happen to me?" We show evidence of growing up, however, when we are able to say, "Sorrow and misfortune come to most of us, but God will see us through. He will make us stronger because we meet life's experience in the spirit of Christ." A preacher in a certain western town stopped in front of a rather dilapidated shack to make a pastoral call. One of the boys stood admiring his automobile. The minister explained to the boy that his brother had given him the car. Then the little fellow said a very real thing: "Gee, mister, I wish I could be a brother like that."

We have said much about the state of security in a home that makes for maturity. Just feeling secure, however, is not the last chapter in the whole story of a life that is on its way to fulfillment. To feel secure may merely mean feeling smug. To feel secure, to realize one's powers, and to know one's worth are not ultimate things. They are highly useful assets in the struggle for common good in the kingdom of God. What parents have sought to do for their growing children meets its real test when they are grown-up and ready to launch out for themselves. It comes at the point of that young person now grown being willing to become a part of the give and take of life, in times of calm and storm, and sharing happily whatever life brings. In fact, a young person will need to grow up ready to risk the very security that he has sought through all his growing years. When a person can undergo the inner experiences of a great abandon to God's cause, in obedience to his summons, then he has found the ultimate in life.

8

Discipline or Do as You Please?

HOW will you handle your children? Sooner or later a home arrives at the policy-making point. Shall parents be harsh, moderate, or "hands off"? Is it to be "the art of applying a soft pedal instead of a hard paddle"?—let them alone or let them have it?

IF YOU DO AS YOU PLEASE

Parents for the most part are pretty badly mixed up in dealing with children at the point of regularizing their lives and behavior. Without thinking much about it, some parents adopt the "do as you please" policy. As a policy it has its points. Adults generally do as they please. It seems all right. While the children are small, this "do as you please" policy is particularly and deceptively assuring. Parents guided by a purely affectional impulse, take down the fences and let the child live as he likes. The little boy is so much happier doing what he wants to do, as you will note from the impulsive desires that are emphasized in this poem:

PLANS

When I grow up
(For I must, you know!)
I'll go wherever
I want to go—

76

> I'll go to the zoo
> Whenever I choose,
> I'll walk in the mud
> In brand-new shoes,
> I'll go to the circus
> Two days straight,
> I'll sleep in the morning
> And stay up late,
> Have turkey and ice cream
> Every meal,
> And squeal as loud as
> I want to squeal,
> I'll have six dogs,
> And three white mice,
> And let 'em all eat with me—
> Won't it be nice? [1]
> —DOROTHY BROWN THOMPSON

Parents who follow this policy may not want to admit it, because it allows them to escape the unpleasant realisms of child-rearing. Surely anything as comfortable as the feeling of allowing your child to do as he pleases must be all right. Some folks take for granted that anything easy is divine. In a tragic situation a man who was undermined by years of doing only what he wanted to do, was too weak to face up to life. As his mother stood by and wept she said, "I always allowed him to do as he pleased, because I loved him." Unconditional permissiveness had seemed the way out.

Howard Whitman was a roving reporter who went about the country inquiring everywhere of parents about the methods they used in bringing up their children and with what results. He reports this interesting case. A mother in Pontiac, Michigan, who appeared before the juvenile court judge said, "I raised my child just the way they said I should. I never punished him for breaking things—I just tried to put things

[1] Used by permission of the author.

out of his reach. I let him do as he pleased, and didn't say, 'no, no,' or 'don't, don't.' But now, Judge, he has turned out impossible to get along with. I have never said 'no' to him, so when I say 'no' now, it doesn't mean anything. He doesn't recognize that anyone has any rights but himself." Then the woman added with a sigh, "Well, I guess I trained him that way." Let's face it. The permissiveness that allows a child to do anything that he pleases is not an expression of affection but of weakness.

Even parents who adopt this "do as you please" standard have their moments of doubt. They may not know exactly why. The sheer fact is that unconditional freedom is anarchy, and anarchy reaps a harvest of thistles. This is illustrated by the facetious story of the mother who sent a note to the teacher saying, "Whatever you do, don't punish Willie. We have never struck him except in self-defense."

A rather arresting line appears again and again in the Old Testament: "Every man did what was right in his own eyes." This sounds like a reasonable kind of individualism, but actually it is anarchy. If you look carefully, you will discover in the context of the Old Testament in each instance, the trouble that arose as a result of this innocent-looking kind of individualism. The strident, self-independence, the "do as you please" practice incapacitates the person for teamwork, for sharing, for the dedication to something more than self. Why is this so? Nurtured on the principle of "do as you please," the child has no light for his way. Left to his own-trial-and error kind of approach to life, he has no creative feeling about right goals, and without help or guiding assurance, he frequently does the wrong thing. Later he flounders badly in an adult world where the principle doesn't work. He often becomes resistant and hostile to anyone or anything standing in the path of his desires.

On the other hand, the authoritarian family is a thing of the past. The authoritarian approach was a kind of closed-shop policy—"do as I say or else." It was not suited to a democratic way of life such as the modern family requires. A story which has gained considerable circulation has a mother saying to her boy, "You must do as I tell you."

He replied, "Why should I?"

The mother found it difficult, but she said, "You must do what I tell you because I have had to do what my mother told me and she had to do what her mother told her."

"H'm," said John, "I wonder who started that silly game."

Authoritarianism, which is the exercise of control from the top, in a family may be passé, but authority is not obsolete by any means. You have to have some starch in the life of the home that is to yield standards whereby a child can find his individual role and work out his destiny. The really serious weakness of this "do-as-you-please" policy is that it usually obtains in a weak home. It leaves the child out on a limb.

The fact is, that "do as you please" is a form of rejection. At its heart is an unconcern for the ultimate results it brings to the child and to society. It takes into account only the immediate satisfaction of letting him do what he wants to do. This is an experience which tends to separate parents from their children. "The need for both acceptance and discipline, and for both love and strength," says Richard McCann, "is emphasized by the observation of psychologists that sheer benevolence and permissiveness can cause anxiety and confusion, especially in a child who is disturbed." [2]

The child feels himself cut off from a supporting relatedness. He is left to go it on his own when he has neither the

[2] Richard V. McCann, *Delinquency: Sickness or Sin?* (New York, Harper and Brothers, 1957), p. 103.

light nor the experience to choose wisely. He therefore feels rejected and insecure—he lacks a sense of solidarity which members of the family normally feel for one another. He needs to have the feeling that each member of the family is accountable to and responsible for the other. Without this sense of oneness with his family, he lacks that feeling of adequacy that is so essential to normal living. This problem of leaving the child to himself is evidently an age-old one. We read in I Kings 1:6, "His father had never at any time displeased him by asking, 'Why have you done thus and so?' " It is the spirit of let-him-alone-entirely that is tantamount to rejection. This form of parental attitude can cause a boy to become anti-social, rebelling against any form of authority since he has grown long since to feel that no one has a right to ask, "Why have you done thus and so?"

DISCIPLINE

A child must experience life—rules and all—on every succeeding age level, if he is to reach maturity. A writer in *Zion's Herald* said, "Thinking that three hours of any movie are harmless for the child but two hours of church and Sunday-school are too much for his nervous system is just bad thinking. Giving him a nickel for the collection and fifty cents for the movies not only shows a parent's sense of value but it is also likely to produce a proportionate giver." There are rules that inlay life for all of us. Certainly health, safety and behavior require them. Margaret Flint, in a novel, has one of the characters reflecting on the past, "Well could he remember the code they lived by, the morale that made the family a coherent entity. They must all go to school; they must be clean in mind and body; they must work hard and not fuss about it; they must pull together all the time, in all things; and they must boil the dish towels every day." [3]

A family cannot survive without rules. Surely as a minimum matter, every child should be expected to tell his parents where he is during the day or during the evening. "Some families can trace their ancestry back 300 years," one person said, "but can't tell where their children were last night."

RULES ARE NEEDED

In fact, the child expects some form of common control, recognizing that this is fair. His is an innate agreement with justice. When polled, a number of youngsters declared for supervision by parents and held that more authority is needed. I quote from Howard Whitman again. In his inquiry of the public mind about child-rearing, he found five youngsters in Baton Rouge who said some interesting things about supervision and discipline. Rosemary, aged eleven said, "Well, children should have freedom, but I don't think to run around at all hours." Diana, aged thirteen said, "I'd like the family to be a sort of club. You know—democratic—so that everybody had an equal voice." Harry, aged thirteen: "Not me, I don't think they should all have the same voice. The parents know much more. All I want is for them to understand how the child feels." Kirk, aged fourteen: "I think what a child needs is strong parents." Diana: "Well, I know another girl. She's thirteen and she tells her parents off. They take it. I don't like that." Melba, who was thirteen, said: "I'd rather have my parents lead me and correct me. I mean, we want to know what we can do, and what we can't do. Even if we break a rule, we want to know we broke it."

[3] Reprinted by permission of Dodd, Mead and Company from *The Old Ashburn Place* by Margaret Flint. Copyright 1936 by Dodd, Mead and Company, Inc. pp. 9-10.

In one city a young mother explained, "My son did something bad, and I let him get away with it. He seemed very disturbed about it and when I asked why, he said, 'The least you could do is to punish me.' He talked as though I was depriving him of something." The person reporting the incident went on to say she was depriving him of the chance to square accounts. These youngsters were voicing a regard for parental guidance as well as a desire to keep their feeling of belonging. These comments also indicate that children have an innate sense of fairness.

LIMITATIONS OF FREEDOM

Parents need to remind themselves again and again that the basis for growing a sound Christian person must rest upon intelligent guidance and discipline. A limited freedom is not necessarily without helpfulness. Freedom may be limited for the good of all within the home or the neighborhood, but by its very limitation, may give a child an assurance of a dependable order with controls that protect him as well as restrict him. In a recent magazine article, a well-known writer tells of her childhood days in the home of her Aunt Lizzie, where she grew up as a child. "Aunt Lizzie, a stickler for order and cleanliness, had not the slightest intention of 'picking and cleaning up after disorderly children.' When we were big enough to reach them, we each had to make our own beds—make them exactly as they should be made. If we rushed with muddy feet upon any immaculate floor, Aunt Lizzie would direct our attention to the mop, and sit placidly in the rocking chair while we cleaned up the mess we had made. . . . Aunt Lizzie held the opinion 'there was no happy home without happy parents, and that civilized adults could not live happily in bedlam.' "

True freedom in behavior and attitude is not freedom from restriction or control, but freedom to useful and fuller living. If a boy wants to drive a car when he is too young, rules can be interpreted in such a way as to make it clear to him that they are not arbitrarily invoked, but are means of achieving the right and fair thing. Rules that are in accord with Christian living set one free in the true sense. A child must learn that you can't be free unless you are right with others and with God.

PUNISHMENT

While the child will appreciate firmness, he will also insist on fairness. We need to examine punishment in this light. Punishment is best administered in the form, of the kind, and in the way that a child accepts, so that it brings about the desired change in his conduct.

To begin with, both parents should be in agreement as to the need and form of punishment. Punishment ought not to be according to the size of your feeling, but of the size of the misdemeanor. Ask yourself what is the reason for the punishment. Is it to put my boy in his place? Is it to relieve my bottled-up feelings? Punishment should be a part of the total experience of the child in the ongoing realization of responsible living. Punishment should be remedial—a learning experience. Life is constructed in reference to cause and consequence. You, as a parent, cannot deny your child this lesson. Be sure, however, that while punishment is administered, love is not withdrawn. Punishment with a consequence of bitterness is a battle without victory. Keep in mind the ultimate goal of the fullness of life and the growth and understanding of values as well as of the conception of self. One other word—to administer punishment is not all of the parents' responsibility. Praise, too, is important. The omission of praise may be seriously traumatic for the child. Perhaps a smile, a pat on the head, or to take him up in your arms if he is tiny—all expressed because he has done some one thing well—confirms him in the idea of doing what is best.

There needs to be recognition for achievement, just as appreciatively and as conscientiously granted as reprimand for wrongdoing. In a remarkable little booklet, Rabbi and Mrs. Jerome D. Folkman relate a rather instructive incident concerning their son, when he was three years old. He had received a little red tricycle for his birthday. He learned how to propel himself about, and found a great deal of satisfaction in what he was about to do. One day, he started off down the sidewalk and disappeared. Since this was the first time he had ever gone out of their sight, his parents were terribly disturbed. When he did finally return, he found himself confronted with unmistakable distress and disturbance on the part of his parents.

"Where have you been?"

"Around the corner on my tricycle," he replied, full of pride in his achievement.

"Who said you could go around the corner?"

The boy's face fell. It had not occurred to him that his parents would be displeased by his achievement. His answer was in the form of a question, "What did you get me the tricycle for?"

Here were a father and mother, facing a rather new situation, a world that propels itself forward by wheel. Here was a child beginning the experience of moving about in that world.

"Certainly we wanted him to learn to use wheels for locomotion. We wanted him to be the kind of a boy that would grow up, mature, become a man—yet the very first time that he embarked on a trip around the block, we gave him a dramatic expression of our utter horror and distress." [4]

THE GROWING LIFE

Authoritarianism in the family is passing. The necessity is upon the family to achieve its ends by consent. Again and again parents plead, "How can I get my boy to do what he should do—to say 'thank you,' to brush his teeth, to hang up his clothes?" In the first place, you will not achieve it all at once. If you lead him to pursue the right way over a long period of time you may secure the desired result eventually. You can't argue him into it. That is certain. Storming at him will not do. Nagging is worse than useless and reveals weakness. Whether you win or lose the element of volition must be protected. So also must authority. But how?

In Harry Emerson Fosdick's autobiography, he tells of the following experience: "Starting for school one morning my father turned to my mother, who was waving him good-by, and said: 'Tell Harry he can cut the grass today, if he feels like it.' Then after a few steps he turned back and added: 'Tell Harry he had better feel like it!'" Fosdick goes on to say that he had called that "the best advice ever given me." [5]

In a sense, what his father said about cutting the grass is not as contradictory as it sounds. Authority needs to be identified objectively with what is right, with what makes for good in life. A child then chooses to be for it or against

[4] Rabbi and Mrs. Jerome D. Folkman, *Democracy and Religion Begin at Home*, Committee on Pulpit Publications, Temple Israel, Columbus, Ohio, 1952, p. 4.
[5] Harry Emerson Fosdick, *The Living of These Days* (New York, Harper and Brothers, 1956), p. 33. Used by permission.

it. A child must come to understand how important it is
not to leave toys at the foot of a badly illuminated stairway,
particularly when grandfather is visiting. When he comes
to realize that on his own volition he is doing a good thing,
he will grow in the meaning of self.

A child grows by choices. We all know that. But they must
be responsible choices, not choices of anarchy. When parents
are able to guide and become a part of the plan or the
problem, a child knows that he is not alone in the venture.
Even though the decision rests in his hands, the child is
inclined to make a choice of the good. There follows growth.
This is the way that vital Christian living develops. You can
call this "discipline by consent."

Self-discipline is a vital part of maturity. Dr. George E.
Gardner, Director of the Judge Baker Guidance Center in
Boston, has said that self-discipline is the only sound answer
to the suffering juvenile delinquent. To quote from Dr.
Gardner: "This means that adults have to be adequate models
of good behavior and that the climate of dignity in the home
and in the school would give the child a sense of trust."

Self-discipline comes about through neither unconditional
permissiveness nor a kind of authoritarianism that says,
"This is a court order." Rather it comes by a kind of ac-
companying spirit on the part of parents that helps a child
know what is expected of him. It comes about through his
wholehearted participation without any sense of fear but
rather with a calm confident assurance. Thus he grows in
wholesome self-determination. In such experiences children
are learning to trust parental guidance as they also come to
see that their choices of the good lead to happy and right
experiences.

9

These Turbulent Teen-agers

WE are "bewitched and bewildered" by the teen-ager. Perhaps we ought to stop trying to prescribe cures for what is wrong with him, and start trying to understand him. Parents here and there in our land are throwing in the sponge in the kind of spirit that says "I give up."

"What are you supposed to do," says one mother, "when a child of fourteen or fifteen acts rebellious—just smile and let him think he is behaving beautifully?" One could go on. What are you supposed to do about Dora who monopolizes the telephone or about the talk that goes on down at the corner drugstore? What can you do about the son who suddenly rebels about going to church? How shall you deal with the daughter who is keeping company with a Catholic boy? Are we wrong, parents inquire, when we ask our daughter to inform us as to her whereabouts? One parent says, "Our boy comes in at all hours and he has been lying about where he goes."

What Parents Say

Wherever you go, parents pour out their consternation and voice their defeat. As never before, the focus of the nation's attention is upon the teen-ager. That in itself is having its devastating effect. What is wrong? For at least a moment, see the situation through the eyes of the teen-ager himself. Richard McCann thinks that "it is not sufficient to know the delinquent's deed; we must know the delinquent." [1]

The adolescent reaches out for what life can give, but he shrinks back from what life demands. At no age does an individual feel quite so insecure.

As Winfred Rhoades said, "If you are not grown up, you escape what you don't want to do." Joshua Liebman once said: "The adolescent at moments wants to return to that well-loved country of his childhood where there was less competition, where everything was given to him. Every new stage of life is a shadowing one emotionally and forces us to build some new adjustment out of broken fragments of our past, out of the precious shards of earlier molds." [2]

In the meantime, the teen-ager is pushed out of the pro-tective, comfortable wings onto the stage to play his part. Actually, he has a good case of stage fright. He tries to brave it out, he becomes almost violently recalcitrant at times, he sounds off in tones of immense self-assurance. Parents are wise who keep their blood pressure down and meet these outbursts with some degree of calm.

One mother, terribly agitated, said, "I am thinking of taking Dorothy to a psychiatrist." "Why?" she said, almost indignantly, repeating my question, "because she refuses to help with the dishes and runs into her room and slams the door." This mother failed to catch the transient nature of her daughter's attitude. What mutineers these teen-agers are. What disdain they have for authority and the due process of home life. You sound the dinner call; ten minutes later

---

[1] Richard V. McCann, *Delinquency: Sickness or Sin?* (New York, Harper and Brothers, 1957), p. 111.
[2] Joshua Loth Liebman, *Peace of Mind* (New York. Simon and Schuster, 1946), p. 42. Used by permission.

this young daughter appears. Scolding does not a modicum of good. As Betty MacDonald put it: "The tricky thing to remember about adolescents is that they are going to be miserable no matter what they are doing, but they would rather be miserable doing the things they choose."

TEEN-AGERS SEEK ACCEPTANCE

Teen-age is a kind of cocoon stage, in which individuality is unfolding, and independence of parental direction and dominance is developing. The pressures to grow up are upon this emerging life. The transition from ego-centered existence to social responsibilities and a multiple relationship is on the way. The teen-ager is inarticulate, self-conscious, uneasy with adults, explosive, and inwardly unsure of himself.

In a very real sense, the hidden urge of teenage life is a deep desire for meaning, for approval. Some astonishing revelations resulted from a poll of high school students reported in the studies made by the Purdue Opinion Panel. Here are the figures: 26 per cent said, "More than anything I want to be accepted as a member of the group that is most popular at school"; 51 per cent conceded that they had tried very hard to do "everything that will please my friends."

Bear in mind that the teen-ager wants to be important to others. Part of the realism in the problem that teen-agers face is that boys and girls are being pushed into a land-scape of adolescence that demands conformity. They must do what teen-agers do in a given school and neighborhood, or face the stigma of insignificance. Hence the rough exterior at times, the disheveled appearance, and the strange vernacular expressions.

The upward shove of the unconscious is toward conformity with a group. Boys and girls normally desire to win the favor of others who make up the social organization that gives them status.

A fifteen-year-old boy explained how he won acceptance by his friends: "I had to show them that I wouldn't punk out in a fight. I had to go into another block and sound out a guy in a rival club. Insult him, you know? So I did and then we fought. I wasted him—messed him up. I had been like on probation with my own group, but now I was accepted, you know? Now I was a down kiddie. Now I had proved myself, I was a regular."

There is nothing wrong or base about the urge at the bottom of all of this, even though the behavior itself may be anti-social. In fact, the desire to be accepted and to be approved is fundamental and indispensable to the building of a sound life—yes, and to the establishing of a sound home. Three fourths of the battle against delinquency would be over if children came into the world sincerely wanted and not subjected to hostility. If they could experience genuine affection, have approval in every good thing, know themselves to be loved, and no matter what they did, accepted—yes, and disciplined—then indeed could children face life courageously and constructively.

This very desire for meaning on the part of the teen-ager is at the bottom of much of the explosive behavior so maddening to his elders. Before you conclude that the whole home is about to be derailed, however, note what the teen-ager is really seeking. He keenly desires a close knit environment that will yield to him a sense of belonging. Home and church need to give teen-agers the possibility of satisfying this deep hunger to belong and to be approved. A newspaper reporter made a study of five notorious criminals. As he examined their lives, he traced their experiences and their crimes from the very outset. He tells the story of Fred whose parents allowed him to grow up through his early years feeling that he was not accepted by them. Fred, when he was about twelve years old, did a fine thing one day, and his mother commended him for it. The boy broke down and said, "This is the first time you've ever approved of anything I have done."

In a recent treatment, Haskell M. Miller says: "The problem is, in a large measure, one of juveniles in a juvenile society. We talk of mixed-up children. Perhaps we ought also to speak of mixed-up parents."

BOY AND GIRL RELATIONSHIPS

When it comes to the matter of relationship with the other sex, there seems to be a dim dawning of understanding about one another on this teenage level. The dating which these youngsters do illustrates what has been said of the desire for security that comes through acceptance. The basic reason for going steady, psychologists and sociologists agree, is that it gives both young people a feeling of security. Here is one person to whom this boy or girl means more than a passing fancy. For the girl it means that there is always someone to be with at dances and parties. For the boy there is someone in whose eyes he has worth, and perhaps even heroic qualities.

There are parents, however, who feel that steady dating is wrong. A girl or a boy is excluded from other twosome experiences that would be broadening and maturing. Knowledge of the other sex should be predicated, they feel, on acquaintance with a number of persons. According to one mother, it is the girls who are hurt in the long run by going steady. A boy can change his mind whenever he wants to, but a girl carries the label of being Otto's "steady" long after a break has occurred between them. She may have to wait an indefinite period before any other boy shows an inclination to be interested in her.

Going steady with one person may present the likelihood of too much physical involvement. A growing intimacy experienced too early in life can prove extremely unwholesome. It is, of course, obvious that parents should not make light of the tone of finality in which their son announces that this is the girl for him. It is important for parents to know the boy that their daughter is seeing. It is necessary, too, to provide the kind of home atmosphere that keeps young people from feeling self-conscious about being together in the presence of other members of the family.

Still more seriously, the boy and girl may determine to marry early. Parents may be right to have an adverse mind on this matter. Little, however, is accomplished by opposing the desire of these young people with vehemence. Keep a positive picture before your boy or girl concerning marriage. Point out that an interest based on a more seasoned insight as to what marriage really means is of the utmost importance.

It is at this point that the teen-ager comes to grips with the subject of sex, and there are relatively few parents who feel "sufficient for these things." Well, we had better be! Do know, however, that facts, just of themselves, are not enough. You may inform your boy or girl very fully concerning sex, its biological meaning, its function—and yet fail. Facts that are related glibly or grossly will only kindle a fire and make for moral anarchy. This a sacred subject. Whoever is to be the informer (youngsters vote again and again that parents should be the persons to give sex understanding) needs to make sure that facts can be presented sanely and soundly and in a hallowed way. The really great need is to relate spirituality to the sex urge, and make evident the fact that sex must always be under spiritual disciplines. Boys and girls need to accept themselves as they are, and to understand that the physical experiences of life can help to make for fulfillment in their own lives and at the same time glorify God's creation.

Parents ought to listen as well as to instruct. "Mother and Daddy just tell us what is what, and that's all there is to it." Dr. C. D. Williams reminds us, "You don't need to be right all the time. Your child wants a man for a father, not a formula. He wants a woman for a mother, not a theory. He wants real parents, real people, capable of making mistakes without moping about it." [3] One hundred fifty thousand youngsters interviewed in one hundred high schools came up with many complaints. For example, they were unable to discuss personal problems with their parents; and many fathers and mothers failed to accept their children as responsible persons. One high school girl said, "I wish I could talk over my problems with my folks, but every time I tell my mother something, she starts giving me a long lecture on the subject."

RIGHT AND WRONG

A greater indictment has come from the findings of the Purdue Panel. More than 50 per cent of the teen-agers interviewed think that the large mass of Americans aren't capable of deciding for themselves what's right and what's wrong. There are parents who leave much to be desired. There was the father who bought a new Buick Roadmaster for his sixteen-year-old son. The next day he frantically called the principal of the high school to inquire if he knew of the son's whereabouts, and whether or not he had played truant from the school. "Where do you think a boy would

[3] *Quote Magazine*, October 9, 1955.

go in a new Buick Roadmaster," asked the principal, "to school?"

Down in Shreveport, Louisiana, the Y.M.C.A. secretary, M. E. Mischler, who has had a vast experience with youth, said: "Those who are causing trouble lack self-discipline and deep moral development. Their parents teach them the niceties and the fine points of etiquette, but give them nothing toward inner development. A good boy has to be taught within as well as without. If he is not, then his goodness is like a coat to put on." When this happens his life is indeed a house built upon the sand. It will fall when the floods descend and the crises come.

A part of the fault lies with parents who have given youngsters very little that helps to condition them toward right and against wrong decisions. We want these boys and girls to be good. If we are to accomplish this, we must have homes with fathers and mothers possessed of a firm, irrefutable morality. Children in such homes tend to make that morality their own.

According to the Yale studies, the majority of the chronic drinkers testified that they began drinking in high-school days. What is even more of an indictment, most of them began their drinking in their own homes. Some years ago a tragic incident occurred in a family. The daughter, twelve years of age, was brought home from a roller rink in an intoxicated condition. Whereupon her father and mother, with no apparent concern for their daughter's drinking, went back to the roller rink only to insist that she be allowed to return to the place for her enjoyment. The latter to them was a far larger issue than the tragic fact of intoxication.

As Christian parents, what are you offering to your teenagers that they can tie to in the way of ideals and life purposes? What do you really want these young people to be and to do with their lives? Are the churches and homes in our modern day giving to young people something that is soul-stirring and spiritually thrilling, as well as liberating? Parents can have clean-cut standards of decency, honesty, and temperance, without being stuffy. Again, the home that exists merely for things and whose major and continuing interest is in material success cannot hope that their children will live primarily for what is sacred and abiding. What are we giving our sons and daughters to tie to, if our ideas of right and wrong are based upon pleasure and profit, if for us to be comfortable is more important than to be holy? There was a sharp line of demarcation between right and wrong in an early day. You didn't gamble, you didn't use foul language if you were Christian.

Organized religion seems to have failed also. There was a time when we proudly boasted that no child in the church school ever found his way into a juvenile court. But look at the record now. Just to be enrolled and to attend church school is not enough. It appears all too often that both church and home have lost their grip.

Evidently the mandate is upon us to define more clearly and to adhere more strictly to the Christian standard by which we shall conduct our lives. Homes need an interlinear purpose that is felt in ways of living, in daily behavior. One more fundamental must be added. When parents maintain consistently a relationship of love, understanding and trust, the children in the home are far more likely to hold on to what is right and good.

10

Every Husband and Wife

THE very least a husband and wife can do is to try to understand each other. It isn't a simple accomplishment. The fact is that the differences represented in men and women are considerable. John Laurence says that "men neither talk, nor think, nor even dream as women do. They are different in love, different in friendship, different in hate." [1] Reputedly, women cannot understand men. One woman columnist writes to say that women find it hard to understand "how a man can be vague about his children's ages and still remember the batting average of every baseball player on his favorite team." Nor can she understand "why a man thinks that his inability to understand a woman is something to brag about." And finally she also wonders, "how a husband can have so much to talk about when he is away from home, and so little to talk about when he is at home alone with his wife."

On the other side, men cannot understand how much a new hat will do to help a woman's morale. Nor can he explain why a telephone conversation can be so long in point of time and of so little importance. Aside from these facetious observations, one can make a good case for the difficulty of

[1] John Laurence, *The Single Woman* (New York, Duell, Sloan and Pearce; Boston, Little, Brown and Company, 1952), p. 171.

understanding one another. Differences are more profound than appear at first glance.

In the marital relation itself, the lack of understanding of each other is part and parcel of the lack of understanding of the institution of marriage. How else account for the fact that divorce is more likely to occur during the second or third year of marriage?

In Christian marriage the important fact is growth. A wedding is an event; a marriage is a life. You grow a successful marriage. Identification of husband and wife, one with the other, becomes more and more enduring and complete as experiences bring about a growing mutual trust and love. As this process of growth goes on, husband and wife develop an increasingly sensitive awareness and appreciation one of the other. The disciplines that come from bearing with each other's difficulties or weaknesses have a maturing effect upon each life. For both husband and wife there is a deepening realization of the meaning of the other within this structure of intimacy. All of these experiences bind two lives more and more closely together.

LITTLE THINGS ARE DESTRUCTIVE

Much of marital failure is due to little things. A brush fire spreads into flames so great that it leaves a formerly beautiful realm of affection nothing but deeply charred and scarred earth. These tragic estrangements and hostilities begin with little infinitesimal things. On the wife's part there is that constant interruption, "You always do so and so . . ." or she may attempt to shut off his criticism with unfortunate success. On his part, the husband may refuse to visit his wife's relatives or he may be utterly blind to the fact that the lady has dressed especially to please him.

Little things bring on the big disasters in married life. Husbands and wives need to develop a spirit of tolerance and a sense of fairness. When each regards his marriage partner with a deepened view of the sacredness of the other's personality, it helps immeasurably in overcoming these little enmities that may grow to amazing proportions. The fact is that marriage ties often reach the breaking point because one or both partners lack the positive mind with its ready willingness to overcome these little irritating evils. Such moods and attitudes destroy a marriage just as often and as surely as the alienation of affection.

Of course little things are not always the direct cause of these marital disasters, but they do reveal the deterioration that is going on. Marriage is not wrecked by a blowout but rather by a slow leak. Marriages are not destroyed by big things. Jim and Mary do not give up each other when the job is lost, or the baby is crucially ill. When the sudden tragedies march down upon our homes, it is natural for married couples to seek divine aid and to give their best help to each other. However, the little evils, deceits, nasty innuendoes, misunderstandings, and neglect seem to emerge when we are not on our guard. Gradually, they bring about ugly erosions in what was once the fair and fruitful land of romance.

The woman who sat in the interview room was the figure of dejection. She slumped over in a chair. After a little while she looked up. "I didn't think he would leave me," she said in a lifeless tone. "He complained about my untidiness. I did realize it in a way, but I never seemed to catch up." There was more to it than that. Her temper outbursts came with increasing frequency. She seemed utterly insensitive to the need for keeping up a happy relationship. All of these things added up to her present picture of desolation.

MARITAL VEGETATION

Little things are not exclusively causal. There is a kind of sour, evil soil out of which these little destructive things come. When a man and his wife take each other for granted, they provide a real breeding ground of marital trouble. In too many cases their awareness of each other has lost all of its force. Some marriages just dribble away—die out in a kind of numbness. When the judge of a domestic court asked a man to specify how he had demonstrated affection for his wife, the husband replied, "Well, I did a lot of remodeling around the house."

As I left New York City on a commuting train one evening, I sat opposite a young couple. Evidently they were returning from their day's work in the city. They were now on their way home. He read the paper. She made three efforts to gain his attention and to engage him in conversation. His only response in each case was a grunt. Finally the train pulled in at their station. He poked her with his elbow and said in a gruff voice, "Come on, we're getting off." I watched them as they walked down the aisle of the train and down the steps to the platform. For a moment I closed my eyes and tried to imagine all that followed. They probably would get into a car parked near the station, drive to the house, open the door, turn on the lights. She would go to the kitchen to prepare the evening meal. They would sit down in the dining room facing each other. At that point the whole view grew too bleak and discouraging. I didn't want to see any more. It was a conspicuous case of marital vegetation.

This living together in a kind of phantom way as far as love is concerned, may go on for years. I saw a sign in the window of a New York shop which read, "Washable flowers!

25¢ a bouquet. Everlasting." Some marriages just go on everlastingly without much point and without either lift or life. Harmless as this may sound, it is nevertheless an evil, and a definite enemy of Christian marriage. Out of a matter-of-fact mentality—"so she's my wife, what of it?"—grows the regrettable presence of neglect. Someone has said that more than one man who has succeeded as a lover has failed as a husband.

The twin evil of neglect is carelessness. Dr. J. Randolph Ray says, "It is my opinion that every home ought to have at least two mirrors; one in the kitchen where the wife can see if her hair is still screwed up in curlers, and one in the hall so that the husband can see the look on his own face when he comes home at night. For the fiber of a marriage is made up of looks and expressions, bright smiles or frowns, small intonations in greetings, and changes in voice. Marriage is made up of the way you treat one another, day in and day out, and not of heroic self-sacrifices, or whether or not you would be willing to lay down your life." [2]

More than one study has seriously attempted to probe to the marrow of marriage relationships that have bogged down. Most of them report two things that handicap the relationship. Wives have become careless in personal appearance. Husbands give no thought as to how they talk or act. These are two of the factors that have contributed to the decay of many marriages. "A three-day stubble of beard," said one wife, "is not any more attractive to me than cold cream on my face is to him."

Thoughtfulness, courtesy, appreciation, gratitude—these have wilted on the vine. I stood one day at a Western Union counter in the railroad station in Washington. A man ahead

[2] Dr. J. Randolph Ray, *My Little Church Around The Corner* (New York, Simon and Schuster, 1957), pp. 216-17.

of me was sending a wire. The clerk, a young woman who evidently was not just a wooden-minded person, said in a bright sort of way to him, "You can say more—you have fifteen words."

He countered, "What shall I say?"

She answered, "You can say 'Thank you' and it won't cost you anything."

THE MOLEHILL OF BICKERING

Bickering, when taken by itself, looks like a little thing. And yet there isn't anything more insidious than bickering. The incessant pecking away at a person for every real or imaginary instance of irritation becomes dangerous business. Its effect upon the other person is like biting down on a nerve-exposed tooth. As time goes on, the husband makes a hobby of collecting his wife's defects, and the wife cannot resist putting the husband in the witness box daily. The constant nagging and fussing of two married persons rubs raw and thin the affection that basically is their protection. Bickering is a symptom of an unregenerate ego which is the real threat to marital harmony.

In short, bickering is sinister because it represents a vacuum somewhere in the marriage relation, a negative spirit that is insufficient to keep two people together. You can't bind two hearts into one with nothing at all. There was that woman on the witness stand who said, "All we had to share was our doubts."

DISAGREEMENTS

Disagreements are another thing altogether. When married people lose the ability to "talk it out," or when disagreeing results in a lovely relationship being strewn in pieces all over the place, the marriage is in real peril. If you are going to quarrel, be sure that something constructive comes of it. This does not mean that husband and wife must always agree. Certainly no one would propose that a successful marriage depends upon one person agreeing with everything the other person may say. "The conception of two people," said A. P. Herbert, "living together for twenty-five years without having a cross word suggests a lack of spirit only to be admired in sheep."

When marriage partners are able to express their differences of mind and when they attempt truly to understand each other, they enrich two hearts mutually. This kind of thing is possible only when the marriage partners live in such unity that their love and respect for each other are greater than any differences of mind that they may face. As someone has put it, "If you agree that it is poor judgment to quarrel before company, remember that two is company." When disagreements do come, by all means stay on the same wave length. Keep the channel open for diplomatic conversations.

In a magazine article entitled, "Intelligent Woman's Guide to a Reasonably Happy Marriage," Sam Grafton makes this statement: "It helps if you and your husband can talk it out. Whether you can depends on the level of communication you have established with your everloving. Sometimes you try to say you are frightened or tired by slamming the crockery in the sink or banging the oven door. It may be hard for your husband to get these messages. It is better to learn how to come out with it and say, 'I'm scared', or 'I'm tired.' It doesn't mean that you are a coward."

Many of us have seen situations in which a husband and wife under trying circumstances strike out at one another in resentment and finally go their separate ways. We have seen another husband and wife who may be facing precisely the same kinds of circumstances but as Christian persons, they are able to talk it through and discover eventually a reason in these circumstances that draws them closer together. If at the beginning of marriage, young couples would pray out loud about their disagreements, ill will would dissolve and the light of divine guidance would bring reason upon the dooming circumstance.

LITTLE THINGS KEEP MARRIAGE SATISFYING

Little things can work positively as well as negatively. So turn this matter around. The right little things can be just as potent in preserving a marriage as other little things are in destroying it. The little act of thoughtfulness and the kindly attitude nurture and strengthen a good marriage. How wise is that wife who insists upon canceling plans for the evening show or concert when she sees that her husband is dog tired. She goes the second mile when she gives evidence of enthusiasm about spending the evening at home. How wonderful is that husband who can sense when his wife has had a rough day and that he can do something about it. When he, therefore, puts aside his own desire and takes her out for an evening together, both of them find a new glow of happiness and sense anew the significance of their relationship.

See the virtue of the thing in another way. A man and his wife are frequently out with the same crowd—the loud talk of her self-opinionated husband is really something to put up with. Or sometimes there is a wife who interrupts her husband's story with those unfortunate contradictions. At first these unhappy instances cause a sense of inner revulsion. Finally a man or a woman may meet them with outright resentment and then both of them harvest the bitter fruit of strained relations. While such unhappy incidents may grate severely on the nerves of husband or wife, they can learn to handle them. When persons meet such issues with tolerance and kindness, they will discover how different the result can be.

It's precisely the little thing that does the trick. Put a note in the one-suiter to be opened on his first night away. Indulge in an extra telephone call just to say something gay or teasing or thoughtful. Little things like these refresh the love of two people for each other. As one writer puts it, "A flower given to your wife for no reason at all is worth a whole carload of Easter lilies."

I have seen a wife to whom it would have meant everything in the world to have had her husband sitting with her in church, even occasionally. I have seen a husband who would have been grateful if, just once in awhile, his wife had been willing to listen seriously to his new idea. Its possibilities so inspired him that he couldn't keep still about it, but she was listless and bored. How tragic!

Strange how the whole game of getting on together goes well because of a kindly spirit expressed in a trying moment. Speak a considerate word or do some simple little thing out of an impulse of affection—and with it comes the feeling, "we belong together."

MARRIAGE AS ETERNAL

Basic to Christian marriage is the concept of marriage as eternal. There are two views of marriage in our modern day. In the first, marriage is seen as an eternal union, so designed that individuals fit into its structure and meet its demands. In the second, marriage is seen as a union that fits into one's individual notions and conceptions of right and pleasure. The latter view is causing our trouble. We are under the necessity of rescuing marriage from what David Cohn called, "A temporary agreement, like buying a stove on thirty-days' trial." This is not the Christian view.

The Christian view makes it explicit that the husband and wife stay together not because parting is legally impossible, but because it is spiritually unthinkable. The couple with that view begins marriage convinced of one thing—that they will never give up their marital relation. Out of that conviction they develop resources that enable them to solve the difficulties as they come day by day. Out of those rich resources they come to believe that a person cannot turn his back on his marriage because to do so is to turn his back upon what is too priceless to surrender. Dr. J. Randolph Ray observes, "Living together is hazardous enough without the added handicap of 'merchandise returnable.' "[3]

The individualism of much of the modern view accounts for the kind of mentality that says, "If you don't like the relationship you have, try another." In Massachusetts a ninety-year-old wife on her wedding anniversary declared, "People don't work at being married these days. They don't realize love is a chore as well as a charm. Back in 1878 when I got married, women were more sensible. We tied our wedding knots with steel then. If a girl found her husband a problem, she worked until she solved him. She didn't shop around for another man like they do now."

If a marriage is to be successful, the union must be real. A marriage will not hold if the husband or wife still gives primary allegiance to a childhood home. They are wise parents who insist that their children, as soon as they are married, shall put their mates first. Only this can create a

[3] Ray, *op. cit.* p. 206.

successful, lasting marriage. This kind of union in the newly established home puts first the loyalty of husband to wife and of wife to husband, though both may love their children dearly.

There is no denying the fact that marriage gains coherence because of physical compatibility. To be harmonious sexually is of great importance, and yet sexual harmony is no guarantee of marital success. We have oversold physical compatibility and undersold spiritual affinity. In more than one instance, it has been found that couples who were well mated, and physically harmonious, were nevertheless facing a dilemma that pointed to divorce. Today we have more information about sex, and apparently more futility in marital relations.

The successful marriage is a marriage of a shared life. Many young married women work outside the home to aid their young husbands in financing their graduate education. More than 26 per cent of the couples living together have double employment. Often the husband shares in the work of the house as they return to their home in the evening.

Finances are likewise to be shared. One woman puts it this way: "To me marriage is a partnership in the highest and most exalted meaning of the word. My husband works and I work, he at his office, I in our home. We earn one combined salary, we pay our bills, buy our necessities, share our meager surplus for amusement."

Supporting this idea comes the testimony of a man who says, "The money I bring home is hers as well as mine, because without her, I could not perform my duties and could not command our income." Absolute equality in the affairs of finance is part of a growing, mutual feeling concerning the values of marriage.

One thing more. Most women need the feeling of independence and the self-confidence that a little money gives.

A small amount in a savings account of her own yields untold satisfaction.

The sharing of life does not mean that two young people live to themselves for themselves. No condition so quickly dries up the springs of attractiveness and inspiration as for a husband and wife to isolate themselves in their own home. Man and wife in their own relationships will, from separate interests, bring much that enriches and refreshes their common life together.

If you want your marriage to grow and achieve a stanchness to stand against the winds that blow, you must be capable not only of loving, but of being loved. A woman wants to know that she has meaning in life—meaning for other people—but particularly, she wants to be loved and needed by one person. A man grows in nobility and integrity when he knows that he is loved for himself by someone who means it enough to identify her destiny with his. A man must be able to love as well as to be loved. A woman must want to be needed by, as well as to need, a mate. A Christian marriage is one in which this deep, affectional feeling is constantly renewed at the throne of grace and made certain by the underrunning consciousness of that union as being absolute.

In a novel by Howard Swiggett, a Mr. Titcomb, looking at his wife, reflects to himself: "I just wish Mr. Rutledge or Mr. Johnson or Mr. Hewitt or some of the other big boys could have a home life like mine. I've seen a lot in my time and though I'm getting old hope to see more, but I never have and never will see anything as pretty as my wife's face and ways. Everything in the world a man could want is in this little apartment." Then he goes on to say—

"Well, you could call it luck, I've always had luck, but I don't know, to me it was just God's hand. . . ." [4]

A critic of Mark Twain once said the greatest line he ever wrote was about the glory of love and marriage. It was in a bit of writing about the death and burial of Eve. Adam is standing at her grave and he lets his mind go over their years together: the Garden of Eden, with all of its richness—their sin and expulsion from the garden—and the fatal strife between their sons, Cain and Abel—their years of hard work. But, thinking of what she had meant to him through it all, he said, "Where she was, there was Eden."

Finally, the utterly indispensable factor is mutual trust. Trust is a great marital word. Hold your wife or your husband by a trust—a real one. Know this, that open faith is better than a closed shop. Some wives rely on a system for keeping track of their husbands. There is a difference between surveillance and holding a man. Hold each other within the heart by the power of a mutual trust. In this same novel by Swiggett, the main character says, at the very close of the book, "A happy marriage is the great builder of character."

⁴ Howard Swiggett, *The Durable Fire* (Boston, Houghton Mifflin Co., 1957), pp. 68-69.

11

The Family and the Fullness of Life

THE family as an institution is here to stay. We are not deciding its existence. We may decide the quality of its life, its performance, its legal status, but not its reality as an abiding institution. The human race will be perpetuated through the family. Customs may change, cultures may come and go, the abode of a family itself may shift from a tarpaper shack to a sprawling ranch house, but the family will still be the family, the basic unit of human life.

WHY THE FAMILY ABIDES

This staying power of the family is in the main due to an undergirding solidarity. At its heart the family has substance that is able to resist decay. This substance or core of the family may be spoken of as its corporate life. The family has its own corporate life—its entity—a life in itself and by itself. The family is more than the sum of its members, somewhat in the same way that a nation is more than the sum of its citizens. The family is the total of its members plus their interactions, one with another—the interplay of their minds and feelings within the frame of family living. In other words, the family by definition must include the living together of which each member is a part. The family is the total of what the members mean together, feel together, do together.

This oneness in structure and form gives the family its nature and its destiny. The intimations of this corporate life are to be found in such expressions as, "The family was home for Christmas," "They never had a family life," "Does he have a family?" We talk about "a broken home"—we say we "don't want to break up the family"—we speak correctly of a family outlook, of family understanding, of family ambition. Not long ago, a popular magazine carried an article entitled, "Does Your Family Have a Neurosis?" The subtitle explained that according to an important new psychiatric theory, the family, just as the individual, can be mentally ill. For example, an individual or a family may be hysterical, compulsive, or mother-fixated. The family as such has an existence of its own.

LET'S CALL IT THE FIFTH JONES

Here is the Jones family, the father and mother and two children—four persons held together within the hand of the home. But actually there are more than four persons when those four persons are a family. The family as such is an additional life over and above the four persons—a "fifth Jones." Why not the "fifth Jones"? The "fifth Jones" embodies the emotional tones and patterns of the behavior of the family. It is this very corporate life, this "fifth Jones," this wholeness of the family, that feeds the emotional life of the child and helps him become mature. Just as proteins, minerals, and other basic foods combine to produce energy and growth in the physical life of the child, so faith, love, and understanding experienced within the family relations feed the spiritual and emotional life of a child. As someone has said, "It's a kind of psychological metabolism."

Once a person is a member of a family, and everyone is, you cannot deal with him in exclusion of his family meaning. He is inseparable from all that breathes and lives in his home. Dealt with separately, he is only a part of a whole. You can't break off a piece of a home and deal with that. If we desire to make religion meaningful to persons we must see each individual in the light of the inherent life of the family. The church seeks to help persons through preaching, teaching, pastoral care, or counseling. As it continues to serve persons, it will do well to think of every one of them as integral with families and homes. Quite generally the church plans a church program for the family. But it must do more than that. It must get the family on its mind and heart. Today's need is for the church to go with the family into the home to make it Christian. The family offers the greatest present-day opportunity for the redemptive work of the Kingdom. Both evangelism and education must lay siege to the corporate life of the home. Let the church become family-minded.

The Modern Family Under Threat

We have been discussing the intrinsic strength of the family. We have been talking about it as a corporate life. We have said that within this corporate life are strengths which stand against the attritions of modern living. There is an eternal nature to the oneness of the family, an indivisible, insoluble oneness. Is there any treasure like the togetherness of a family? Like the togetherness of a father, a mother, and a child? This togetherness is made up of cooperation, common activities, loving and being loved; all pervaded by a spiritual power, a kind of eternal sanction from the heart of God. On its homelier side, this togetherness comes about through a common joy in everyday interests. This is how one youth saw it, "This means that Pop washes the dishes before he starts building the porch furniture so that Mother can get her P.T.A. telephoning done in time to drop Junior at the Scout meeting on her way to the textile paint class."

And yet these very activities of the family offer a problem. This priceless oneness we have been talking about is under threat by reason of the overwhelming burden of the activities that a family seems to take on.

Lure of Community Activities

The average American community is a veritable merry-go-round. You get on for a social ride at the point of any number of club meetings, civic rallies, testimonial dinners, and you've had a ride—and that's about all. All your time is scheduled for you. Have you ever scanned the national calendar of special interests? There is National Smile-Week, Snow-Tire Week, Eat-Cheese-and-Butter-Week, Tea-Bag-Week, and others. Consumed as we are with community meetings, auxiliary bake sales, social projects, and literary papers, it is rather hard to build family life on the foundation of the simple graces and integrities that come from living together. To add to our dilemma, our children have become junior joiners. The community leaves no rallying place for the family. You cannot have fullness of life for the family with what is left over after the community has drained off the energies and loyalties of its members.

MATERIAL THINGS AND THE HOME

The home is under the threat of the importance we grant to material things. Our city culture is doing something to us. Strange forces are working us over. Life is evolving us into a new plot. We are players taken from a drama of the past and put into new and more secular roles. The importance of things seems to have moved onto the center of the stage in the home. We have not deliberately given up God, but in many homes God is no longer at the center of existence. What we have done is to lift the finite up to the level of spiritual importance. Many homes are more concerned with being modern than being eternal. We are told that in a few years, all the groceries and commodities needed for the maintenance of the home will be viewed on television. Following the selection made by push-button action, the goods will be delivered at the door. We are told that when housewives are downtown shopping and it begins to shower, they will be able to telephone their homes, and an apparatus attached to the phone will automatically close the windows for protection against the rain. To come to the point of the matter, all of this absorption in the dazzling possibilities of new conveniences and interesting contrivances for the home does not spell fullness of life for the family. Emotional and spiritual needs cannot be met with material means. We lose the whole game when we attempt this.

The secularity of our day seems to be in a gigantic conspiracy against any preoccupation with spiritual life or values. Buying gadgets for the home becomes an obsession. The forces of huckstering have been reinforced by television. John Keats, commenting on this, says, "A recent advertisement . . . showed a family grouped around a glowing television set in the foreground, a washing machine spinning in the background. Your washing machine, the ad said, is working for you, washing and drying your clothes so you won't miss a minute at your television set—where no doubt, the bemused family find still other gadgets for sale." [1] All of this may be modern man's misguided, pathetic self-deception that causes him to go stumbling about trying to find the fullness of life for himself and for his home in the wrong place.

FULLNESS OF LIFE FOR THE FAMILY

Much of what we have been discussing resolves itself into the question of how we can rescue the family from the deteriorations of secular and superficial existence. How can we bring the American family to realize that right here within itself are the spiritual resources that make possible the fulfillment of their deepest desires and their inmost longings? Out of its harmony, out of its common seeking for God's love and light, will come the fullness of light for the family.

Again let it be said that now is the time for the family to realize the richness of its life through being together as members. A woman was reflecting on life and all of its open doors to rich living in the immediate present. She thought of a wool dress that she once bought, "a French hand-knit original." She prized it so much that she rarely wore it. She was keeping it for special occasions. One day she took it out of the box only to find that it had been partly destroyed by the moths. We are like that. We go along in such an utterly matter-of-fact way in our family living that we lose our chance to live fully.

Innumerable times at funeral services a minister hears some friend or a member of the family say of the deceased person, "He was just beginning to have things nice." Or,

[1] John Keats, *The Crack in the Picture Window* (Boston, Houghton Mifflin Company, 1956), p. 87.

they may say, "She was just getting to the place where she really could enjoy life." What a comment on our failure! Our possibilities for living abundantly are constantly present in the family at any stage of its life. The family relationship helps us to find the deepest meaning of life and in such a treasured way. The challenge to the family from the very beginning is to live now. You can have all the graces and the goodness of God to make your life full and rich. The greatest hazard for the family at this point comes from the fact that it is all so close to us that we can't, with any degree of vividness, feel its life and power.

If family living is frittering away, crumbling under tension, graceless because of scattered interests, let it be strengthened and refreshed by renewed dedication. How can persons so intimately bound together, who experience the same ills and the same good favor, live together without meaning or joy? How can they move on from one day to another without realizing and welcoming God's light breaking through into their common lot? To live the Christian way in our homes is certainly to be liberated from dullness and mediocrity.

That Family Feeling

This fuller life that we have been talking about arises from a family feeling primarily—a warmth that unmistakably moves through the minds and hearts of the family. There is something about a family feeling!—that is, when you come to think about it. Few of us ever do. Members of a family have certain inner feelings about one another, about that little, but important world of family living.

There is an interesting book entitled, *Dying We Live*. It is an anthology of the messages and letters sent back home by

persons who were condemned to death by the Nazis. One
young woman wrote to her family, "Today is a beautiful day.
You are somewhere in the fields or in the little garden. Do
you feel as I do that fragrance, that loveliness? It is as though
I had had an intimation of it today. I was out walking, I was
in the open air, which was full of the essence of spring, of
warmth, the shimmer and scent of memories. The naked
nerve of the soul was stirred by the poetry of the commonplace, the smell of boiled potatoes, smoke and the clatter of
spoons, birds, sky, being alive—the everyday pulse beat of
life. Love it, love one another, learn love, defend love, spread
love. So that you may perceive the beauty of the obvious gifts
of life as I do—that is my wish for myself. So that you may
be able to give and to receive." [2] In the hour just before
death came to this young woman, the simple things stood out
in memory. They represented the wondrous life of her home.

The family feeling is the impact of the lives of its members,
one upon the other, storing up sweetness and strength in the
memory and life of each. A family feeling is the unspoken
communication of life to life, within a relationship unique and
exclusive. This family feeling comes as a result of years of
living together, weeping together, laughing together, dream-
ing together, hoping together.

Gladys Hasty Carroll, in her very remarkably vivid way,
depicts a family scene in one of her interesting Maine novels.
It was the Brown family. "Here were people who talked as
sap runs, steadily but slowly, and softly, ... There were
many words but no confusion; eating with no sound of eating,
no clatter of knife and spoon, no thud as mugs were set down;
laughter without noise, more like music. . . . And Browns
could be merry without laughter. They could be quiet without

[2] *Dying We Live*, edited by Helmut Gollwitzer, Kathe Kuhn, and Reinhold
Schneider, translated by Reinhard C. Kuhn (New York, Pantheon Books,
1956), p. 70. Used by permission.

silence, without seeming grim or sad or absent-minded. Their eyes laughed; their lips spoke, even when their tongues were still. . . . Browns could touch one another without putting out a hand. Their glances touched, warm and tender. . . . Here hearts were strung around a table, in a small circle of lamp-light, on a chain so fine-wrought you would have thought a lifting breath of air would break it . . . yet nothing ever broke it. . . ." [3]

A family feeling comes from untying knots in tiny shoes, sitting at the bedside of a loved one in pain, keeping the cookie jar on the shelf well filled. Kathryn Glennon quotes someone as saying, "One of the things I'll never forget, if I live to be an old man, is the cold, windy days when we get in after school and the cocoa is all made and the table is set for a warming party. The cups warm our hands, the cocoa warms our stomachs, and it makes a warm feeling all over." A family feeling grows out of an expressed affection, doing things together, a degree of pride about the family, the exercise of common respect on the part of all.

This family feeling is a universal phenomenon. Some years ago I stood on the corner of one of the main thoroughfares of the city of Kiev in the Ukraine. Across the street a mother was wheeling a baby carriage. She stopped again and again to pick up a rattle thrown out by the baby. I watched as each time she shook the rattle in the face of the child in mock anger. All the while her warm smile betrayed her real feelings. I said to myself, "I've seen that in London, in Paris, at the crossroads everywhere." Her gesture was the universal gesture of the joy of motherhood.

A war widow in Korea was faced with the necessity of giving up one of her children because she could not support all of them. Here was a young mother torn with the anguish of choosing one of her children to be given away to someone else to rear. In her face was written the tragedy of mothers across the world who must be separated from their children or who, keeping them, must arise day after day to find there is no food with which to answer their hunger. Mothers all over the world suffer like that.

In Sarawak, Borneo, last winter, we observed the children of the Dyaks studying their lessons seated about a table in a mission station far up a jungle river. I saw a father with his tattooed body, his black hair cut long over his forehead, and only a decade removed from life as a head-hunter. He stood beside his boy, his hand on his shoulder, and his face beaming with pride. We have seen that everywhere. Joy, sorrow, pride —these are some of the elements of universality that characterize the experiences of the family. The family is historically and universally basic to life!

When this family feeling is rooted in the common faith in the eternal, it gives each person a feeling of well-being and confidence that becomes a defense against the threats of modern hostilities. For the Christian family, this sense of togetherness is an experience of the inner life. It rises up from the level of God's will and God's love. Springs of divine affection refresh the family daily. The love of God becomes an inseparable part of the love of the members of the family for one another. When the experience of growing closer together in the family becomes an experience of growing closer to God, then you have a family that need never fear the ravages of modern life. And it is this shared life based on something beyond the family itself that makes children in the family feel secure.

As a family, turn to the abundant grace and goodness of God as your resource, and live fully now.

12

At Home With God in Your Home

THE family used to pray, and we fathers, mothers, wives, husbands, must pray again. After a sermon on the home a pastor invited his people to sign cards indicating a desire to have their homes dedicated to God. Among the cards that were returned were some that carried additional comments. They said, "I came from a home like that," or "My father's voice in prayer in the morning is still with me in memory." Without hesitancy I offer family religion as a "cure all." Here is our hope. The couple that keeps faith with God, that worships together, that prays together, shall remain strong. The family that worships together in church, that together believes, trusts, and prays, creates a family unity that cannot be broken.

> "So long as there are homes where fires burn
>   And there is bread;
> So long as there are homes where lamps are lit
>   And prayers are said;
> Although people falter through the dark—
>   And nations grope—
> With God himself back of these little homes—
>   We have sure hope." [1]

[1] Taken from: *Light of the Years* by Grace Noll Crowell. Copyright 1936 by Harper and Brothers. Used by permission.

FAMILY PRAYING MUST BE INTENTIONAL

In the old days, when nearly every family engaged in agricultural pursuits, everything that was done on the farm, in the home, in the community, was an invitation to meditate upon God's ways. For many devout persons God was central in every act and will, in every hope and plan, in the early days of our rural economy. Growth and harvest came about through sunshine and rain which were the gifts of his providence. Our parents and grandparents lived with the knowledge that God was in our world. Yes, and more than that, God was in their homes and in all the close-up facts of their living. In the days that are passed, many persons depended upon a clear, cool spring of water to supply their needs. It is hardly possible for a thoughtful person to drink from such a fountain of nature without having a deep sense of the wonderful way in which God provides for his people.

We now live in a culture and context of life where we seem to answer all of our needs through our own creativeness. We tend to forget the original source of water when it comes through city tanks and pipes. God doesn't seem so necessary to our well-being. We now talk about being able to control the rains, conquer space, and achieve any travel speed desired. We are even competing with God, hurling our little man-made worlds into space. God doesn't seem to come to mind very frequently. Pain and suffering, adversity and death, are disorderly intruders. We attempt to meet them with cushioned and padded defenses of frequenal or a bottle of bourbon. God seems so remote. "All that I do all day long," said a very fine Christian person, "seems to stand against a life of prayer." Spiritual things look as though they are a waste of time. Now all that happens in the modern home makes one aware of budget plans, electrical appliances, insulation, and automatic sprinklers. A built-in electric oven and a refrigerator with a two-way door may have importance, but these importances are totally unrelated to God or character. Our homes have suffered tragically from the invasions of secular living. We preserve the outer surfaces of our homes, but we don't know how to renew our inner resources. We take courses in interior decorating, but we have lost the art of beautifying the inner life. Only when the triumphant spirit of God abides in the hearts of the family can we recover these spiritual levels of living.

How deceptive life has become! Our need of God is greater than ever. Fears have grown so monstrous that many people feel insecure. A feeling of deep loneliness overcomes us frequently. Often there is a dwindling sense of personal worth. All of these are the result of remoteness from God. Yet, these very distresses can best be met when we feel at home with God in our homes. Faith, trust, love, understanding, are still the forces that we live by. They are necessary to the adequacy and soundness of family living. These come, with all their refreshing power, only as we maintain unbroken fellowship with our heavenly Father.

A family needs to plan the prayer life of the home intentionally. It will take purpose to bring about the establishment of Christian living in the homes of America. The materials, the literature, the techniques necessary for religious life in the home are available. What is lacking is the will to use them, the will to be spiritual parents, the will to acknowledge openly and gladly our love of God to one another within the family. All of this awaits the intentional commitment of each one of us to a definite plan that includes the worship of God daily in the home. We need to plan as definitely the time and the way for meeting this great need in our lives as we plan for meals, recreation, and rest.

The family needs to pray as a family to develop, to maintain, and to strengthen the spirit of unity among its members. Keeping the family as a whole, close to the heart of God, is one of the ways of keeping the family.

IN TIMES OF CRISIS

These very secular conditions that prevail in our culture are an argument for keeping close to God. There are hazards of travel and traffic. There are social perils in this day of easy morals which endanger and tend to make superficial the lives of your children. Many pressures are upon teen-agers —dates, late hours, and country-club engagements. The fears and feelings of losing out beset us. Then someone says, "I guess we have forgotten God." Prayer empowers a family. A young man and a young woman as they live through that first year of married life together discover the rough edges in one another. They may become impatient; they may say bitter things. If, however, it is their habit to turn to God in prayer, they learn how to dissolve ill-will. Healing of heart and mind comes as they seek and find divine guidance.

Take the family where parents have experienced increasing impatience with a growing boy. He breaks out with what seems to them to be sheer wilfulness. "Why, he is not like our son at all, whatever has happened to him? Tom doesn't come home when he promises. He breaks in on conversations and he refuses to go to bed at a reasonable hour." In their extremity the parents decide to pray. While they pray, realizations sweep over them. The father recalls that he was like Tom at that age. The father and mother together face up to the necessity of being the kind of parents who can learn how to be tolerant and understanding. "Tom is trying to find himself. This is a growing-pain experience." And what about

Tom? As certain changes take place, Tom begins to feel that Dad and Mother are swell about it. He catches his balance in a new climate of security and well-being.

It doesn't seem a crucial matter to have prayer together in your home—and yet it is. Prayer can be the great healer. To neglect prayer will not mean a foreclosure on the house you live in, but it may mean the foreclosure of the home you have come to live for. Prayer is the answer. It helps a family find the answer to its difficulties in the midst of crisis. Continuous, not spasmodic, prayer is a necessity for the kind of family living that takes God into account. That's a reasonable conclusion.

Prayer for Everyday Needs

It is in the vital experience and atmosphere of family prayer that members of a family grow in power to meet the needs that arise in the process of living together day by day. Try to see through their eyes the life story of each member of your family on any single day. Observe the irritations, the embarrassments, the stiflings, and the embitterments. And then let that family unite in a time of quiet worship. As they do, they may sense an inflow of assurance that only God can give. Members of the family may take turns from day to day in reading from the Bible. As one member of the family reads, all may worship as they listen: "I will never leave thee nor forsake thee," "He calleth each one by name," "We are more than conquerors through Him that loved us," "The eternal is my refuge." While we read the Holy Scriptures together, the quiet forces of God's strength are infiltrating the heart. The divine will begins to work its restoration.

AT HOME WITH GOD IN YOUR HOME

The first premise of family worship is an at-homeness with God. Some parents will need to get better acquainted with Him themselves if He is to be invited into the fellowship of the family. Be at home with God in your home!

When you make prayer a part of the normal life of your home, you aid each member of the family in developing an increasing awareness of God. To be at home with God in your home, think of him as a friend. Think of God as a very intimate and wonderful friend, one who cannot come often enough, or stay long enough to please you. Think of him as a friend who quickens the mind, inspires loyalty, and draws out the best in each one of you. Then ask yourself who is the finest person you know, the greatest friend you have. You wouldn't look up that friend just when you were in trouble or when you were in need. You wouldn't insist that he visit in your home only on Sunday morning. You would crave for yourself constant fellowship with such a friend.

If you are to be at home with God in your home, God will need to be more important than all else in the home. Perhaps many parents need to recognize that they have failed to put God first. If a recording device could be hidden in the average church home, recording both what is thought and what is said for the period of one week, what do you think would be the result? Your favorite television program, your golf score, your art lesson, the grades at school, the stamp collection, your rose garden, your furniture arrangement—would these hold the stage of your thinking? If you want to know God, and if you want to feel inclined toward family prayer, you will need to make God the most important part of the life of your home.

Listening to God

Prayer is a two-way experience. We respond to God and God responds to us. In family prayer, ask God for grace to get on together, to love one another when each one knows the worst about the other. Ask Him for insight and calmness in the midst of your private desperations. Be courteous enough, however, when you have finished talking to God, to listen quietly to what he has to say to you. So much of our praying is not, "Speak, Lord, for thy servant heareth," but "Hear, Lord, for thy servant speaketh."

In conversation with your best friend, you aren't absent-minded or preoccupied when he talks with you out of his heart. Yet too often we listen to God with very divided attention. We are much like that disturbing individual at a social gathering who is looking past the person who is trying to talk with him to someone or something else on the other side of the room. Our inattention to God is a discourtesy. You will not hear his voice during your prayer, if you're wondering whether or not you can make the old car do. If, while you attempt to pray, you are trying to estimate whether or not you will have time to make the cake for the bake sale, or whatever will you do about Jimmy's marks at school, you are following God from afar. You are too far off to hear him speak to you.

Try silent prayer as a family. Rapport with God can be instantaneous and complete when the praying is done in silence. Silent prayer bypasses wordiness, it frames its expression in simple and direct language. You can't be loquacious while praying in silence. In silent prayer you know you are either praying or not praying. Sometimes at the evening meal, just join hands and sing, "Praise God from whom all blessings flow." Or sing together one of the reverent prayer hymns your child has learned at church school. These are the things that relate a family to God and to each other.

Daily at the close of the morning or evening meal, read from the Bible and from *The Upper Room* for the day. From time to time make use of other good devotional books including *The Methodist Hymnal,* the *Book of Worship* and appropriate songs and prayers from the church-school material that the church provides for your child. Then join your hands as a family in silent prayer. Give everyone a chance to suggest what has been on his or her heart that he wants to bring to God in prayer. Sometimes this may be a time of praise and thanksgiving when we mention what we have seen and done that helps us feel God near. Or, after burdens and needs are mentioned, let each member of the family pray silently to God for his judgment and help.

While you listen to God as a family, the tide of spiritual strength comes in refreshing the shoreline of the spirit, affirming one's selfhood, removing the sense of guilt and revivifying the oneness of your life together. You may want to conclude silent prayer with the Lord's Prayer, the twenty-third Psalm, or one of the Collects.

START YOUR PRAYER LIFE NOW

We have been talking about homes sustained by prayer. Begin in your home with a realization of the multiplied blessings for which you can be grateful. Note the words of Robert Louis Stevenson's prayer: "Lord, behold our family here assembled. We thank Thee for this place in which we dwell; for the love that unites us; for the peace accorded us this day; for the hope with which we expect the morrow; for the health, the work, the food, and the bright skies, that make our lives delightful; for our friends in all parts of the earth, and our friendly helpers in this foreign isle. Let peace abound in our small company. Purge out of every heart the lurking grudge. Give us grace and strength to forebear and to persevere...." [2]

Perhaps you would like to express to God the feeling you have about your home. If so then you may find inspiration in the prayer of a newspaper columnist which ran as follows: "Resurrect in our minds and hearts the love of the old-fashioned American home with its deep loves and understandings, its family altar, its respect for parents. Restore the sense of values that made a faded picture on a living room wall dearer than the latest Hollywood "super-duper"; help us re-create the mood that saw in a mother's shawl beauty beyond the luxuries of the swankiest boulevard windows. Bring back the spirit of home life in which there rules love and faith and beauty which no world of make-believe could lightly challenge!"

How are you going to have a home like that? Family religion calls for spiritual dedication. It calls for a sense of stewardship about the home, about the way you think, and about the quality of conversation to which you expose your children. Begin now with the practice of prayer. It may seem awkward at first. You may have to change things to do it, but it will change you and your family if you do. Every family needs cleansing from little wrongs, the confirmation of the eternalness of marriage, the forgiveness one of the other. Nothing can take the place of these experiences in our effort to live daily as Christians. Such experiences can come about only through the daily nurture of a spiritual quality in our lives. This is the formula for the growth of sound Christian personality so necessary for our common survival in a difficult day.

[2] Ralph L. Woods, ed., *A Treasury of Inspiration* (New York, Thomas Y. Crowell, 1951), pp. 243-44.